The Government is Not a Village:
Early Childhood Education Policy

Sharon Sarles

Organizational Strategies + Austin, Texas

Copyright © 2014

All rights reserved. No part of this book may be reproduced or transmitted in any form or by any means, electronic or mechanical, including photocopying, recording or by any information storage and retrieval system, without written permission from the author, except for the inclusion of brief quotations in a review.

"Scripture quotations taken from the New American Standard Bible®, Copyright © 1960, 1962, 1963, 1968, 1971, 1972, 1973, 1975, 1977, 1995 by The Lockman Foundation. Used by permission." (www.Lockman.org)

"Scripture quotations taken from the Amplified® Bible, Copyright © 1954, 1958, 1962, 1964, 1965, 1987 by The Lockman Foundation. Used by permission." (www.Lockman.org)

Sarles, Sharon D.
  The Government is Not a Village
  p. 34 cm. 22.5
Includes bibliographical references.
ISBN: 0-9657770-7-3

1. Early Childhood Education 2. Governmental Policy
   3. Education policy 4. Parenting 5. Self-esteem 6. Education – Christian 7. Child care – United States
LC # HN 59.2 S15 2015
Dewey # 362.712

Organizational Strategies, P.O. Box 971, Cedar Park, Texas 78630

www.orgstrat.net   www.thegovernmentisnotavillage.com

Contents

Chapter One :   Let's Talk 1

Chapter Two: The Government is not a Village 22

Chapter Three: What Kind of a Village? 32

Chapter Four: Chelsea's Lunch 65

Chapter Five: Shovels for Sewage 72

Chapter Six: Self-Esteem, Evaluation, and Judgment 87

Chapter Seven: What Kind of Education is Out-Performing? ..103

Chapter Eight: Ideas for Transformation 112

Chapter One
Let's Talk

Children were in crises in the mid-nineties for lack of whole families, lower than necessary IQ, lack of early childhood education, lack of health, and as victims of crime. The First Lady Hilary Clinton points out these conditions and invites us into a dialogue in her book "It Takes a Village." Not uncharacteristically given her lifelong service in law, government, and politics, she suggests government policy and programs might be of some help with these serious problems. Not surprisingly, also, many waved away her suggestion saying, 'NO, it takes parents!" Clinton clearly said early in the book that parents are primary, but she correctly asserts that the nuclear family is supported by many adults doing the right things around and beyond the family. A decade later, the problems are if anything, more severe. I accept the invitation to dialog. Let's talk. Let's first be sure we understand what the problems are, and then let's talk solutions.

We desperately need a way forward, yet we are locked in a deadlock between the red and blue. The Christian gospel and the Kingdom thinking that our nation was founded upon, and the creative impetus that our nation is known for, can offer us hope that is being overlooked and ignored. The dialogue in this country has been degraded into two spun monologues. New ideas and creative energy are sucked into the strife-lock. Children cannot wait. There are answers. When we see one, let's implement it. But let's not implement more of the problem on blind assumption.

Although Clinton brings up many problems, and in no apparent order, let's try to condense the concern down to just a few. It seems that her concerns are poverty, lower intelligence and academic achievement, and finally poor health. I wish to bring up one additional item: character development. Of course, these concerns overlap each other considerably, and each has some sub-parts, but in an effort to be clear and constructive, rather than merely drumming up feeling, let us attempt this organization.

By the way, I have noticed the tendency to "energize the base" rather than "address the problems" or dialogue. Both camps seem happy to raise emotions, present only a part of the issue, and then attempt to mobilize political workers. There is a huge built-in logic for two parties locked in strife to do this. It might be a way to win elections in a two-party system, but it is not the best way to solve problems – or to win others over to your side. Instead, let's address the problems, as well as we can, allow for some points on both sides, and some crowd-sourcing of solutions. Of course, since I am writing a book, I will suggest what occurs to me   When I am blogging, the crowd could point out facets of the problems and alternative solutions. Unfortunately, however, what often occurs is argument devolving to snarky coup-counting. In real life, however, the one with the most friends and the most implementation wins. So let's start talking to one another and let's start implementing solutions. Winning elections will be small potatoes compared to saving a generation.

Let's proceed to getting some shared background on the problems. We do have problems. To deny them is not to solve them. To dislike someone else's solution is not to solve them. Not all suggested solutions solve the problems. It is unlikely however, that we can solve them if we do not know what they are, so in accepting Clinton's invitation, let's talk about the problems.

Poverty

We have about 15 % or so of our population in poverty, using the admittedly somewhat arbitrary official poverty line. Constructed by the federal government based on a basket of goods, mostly food, without considering regional differences in housing prices or non-cash benefits, in 2013, the poverty line is $23,550 for a family of four in the contiguous United States. Therefore, today 15% of the US population, and 20% of its children, fall under the poverty line. Right now, due to poor economy, the percentage is up from the normal 13%. If families took in poor relatives, the line might be down, particularly for small children. In 2011, child poverty reached record high levels, with 16.7 million children living in food-insecure households, about 35% more than 2007 levels. Clearly the problem is worse than during the Clinton era nineties. The rate was worse before 1965. Today, however, since we have more people in the country, the absolute number of people in poverty is higher. The percentage of children is much higher, due to the dramatic increase in single female-headed households.

We have the highest percentage of children in poverty of any industrialized country. The biggest chute down into poverty is to be young, female, not yet educated, from a family that won't or can't rescue you, and then have children out of wedlock. It is nigh onto impossible to get out of poverty from there. To get out of poverty, one needs to get a good job; and to get a good job one needs either a college education or some special talent, along with some time to work hard. These are normally obviated when one has children. Further, children cost money, as well as time and attention. If you ignore children to focus on work and education, then normally you have damaged children. It is difficult.

Currently in the United States, 35.7% of the children born are born to unwed mothers, according to the Census Bureau. More women will face single parenthood due to divorce. Women who have children while not married are more likely the younger and poorer ones; but increasingly, this is a middle-class phenomenon as well. There is probably some slack in the data, in that some are coupled but not married. Nevertheless, this is a fundamental problem, one that Clinton points out. Unfortunately, this statistic is worse than two decades ago, and the rate of increase is increasing. One significant thing that has changed is that today a larger proportion of young women see nothing wrong with bearing children out of wedlock.

Given that we have half the number of divorces as marriages each year, and normally the mother is given custody, and divorcing mothers nearly always lose economic status, then a high percentage of our children end up being poor at some time in their lives.

Minorities have a higher rate of poverty than European-Americans, with native born African-Americans having the highest rate. Nearly half of all African-American children are born to unwed mothers, and 70% of them will live in a single-parent household at some time. Nearly half of African-American children live in poverty at any given time.

Living in poverty is the root cause of other problems for children. Lack of food and poor food quality impact IQ and health. Living in a poor neighborhood almost always means that one attends one of the poorest public schools, and has the highest neighborhood crime and lowest economic opportunities. There may be access to "health care," but it also is of the poorest quality. Further correlates are disorganized families, lower aspirations, and sometimes fewer public services. Stress correlates with everything bad.

For a high-income country, and still at this point the world's largest economy, we have a strangely high percentage of our people in poverty. Some argue that this is because we are less socialistic. Others argue that, given our unique set of diversity, socialistic programs have exacerbated the problem. Others argue that we have too much or too little free enterprise (which, please notice, is not the same thing as bureaucratic capitalism). It is more than a tautology to say that the United States has a higher poverty ratio because it is a more diverse country. We have new immigrants at a higher rate than most countries, and these newcomers are predictably less integrated into the economy. Further, the history of slavery and discrimination has left portions of our population in poverty, in depressed areas, and with damaged mindsets. Further, our great diversity of ideas, history and regions opens the door to ongoing poverty – as well as dramatic rises in wealth – in a way that a more homogeneous country would not experience. A country like Japan has some homogeneity inbuilt, even without socialistic policies; they also have some cooperation between government and business. Germany has a more homogeneous society – not counting their guest workers. This perhaps leads to their ideas of solidarity, and therefore socialistic policies. We, by contrast, founded in freedom, have always been more individualistic. Further, we do have some socialistic policies, some of which are not taken into account by the poverty statistics. For instance, non-cash subsidies are not considered. Therefore, someone whose housing, food and healthcare is paid for may still be counted as having only a few dollars of income – perhaps some family contribution. Historically, we have considered the freedom to be diverse as an acceptable, possibly even good, thing. Yet, today, this diversity of income is considered an evil in itself and certainly a drag on the overall economy.

Imagine if we could tax the rich enough to give everyone in the country $30,000 a year. Would we still have poverty? Of course, we could *not* do this because the rich already complain, get variances, and leave. We also cannot do this because we have already spent far too much on this and other programs, and are going forward mostly on debt-servicing. However, in our thought experiment, at this writing, $30,000 is above the poverty line for a family of four and in my town would provide a decent living. Statistically, this should eliminate poverty. But would it really? Would costs for rent or foodstuffs go up? Would we have no children with IQ, achievement and health problems? Would some spend the money unwisely? Would others make more babies? Could someone run a computer simulation? We would like to know.

I do think that perhaps some margin would be greatly improved. In some families, where they get no aid but rather claw for achievement crumbs, there would be great relief. There might be some families who could then scrape together enough for a business, and some of those would make it. Unfortunately, however, I think we would see inflation on prices of ordinary items, a lot of foolish spending, and continued problems.

President Johnson's War on Poverty worked by every statistical measure. More people went to school, got good jobs, and the percentage of people in poverty dropped for a while. Some would argue that it simply was not continued long enough. Others point to differential fertility rate and an increased entitlement attitude, and suggest that the program created more poverty. Experts disagree. Certainly sexual mores changed at the same time. At any rate, even though poverty is a root cause of our difficulties, there seems to be no quick fix for poverty. In this direction. Johnson's program, along with war, was too expensive; and today, we have not only no money but no credit.

Statistics, even the most optimistic from Keynesian economists, clearly indicate that "a rising tide" does NOT float all boats. The median income has risen steadily for the past forty years, but the poor remain in poverty. The rich are getting very much richer, and some of the upper middle-class are getting rich; and the middle class may appear to be getting more money, but the working class and the poor have not increased their household income over forty years of median income increase. In point of fact, the middle class is greatly squeezed, and many have fallen into lower middle class. We have a higher percentage of people dependent on public funds. We all know about unemployment, disappointed workers, and underemployed people – and people who no longer have pensions. We have more middle-aged white men on SSI than at any time previous – five times more than in the 1960s. Is work that much more dangerous? Are men that much sicker? Is there that much more entitlement mentality? The actual factual situations are usually a lot more complicated than most people wish to admit.

Furthermore, the bigger pictures of the world market and monetary system are not as favorable to us as they were sixty years ago. Macro-policies will clearly negatively affect our poverty rate going forward. There is no question, however, that policies that would encourage work and entrepreneurship would create less poverty than programs that make for dependence. Further, there is no question that better education, and presumably more, would make for less poverty. The question is not which ladder to build, but how best to build it. The ladder out of poverty may be built from both sides, so rather than continuing to battle it out ideologically, it is time to find commonality, real numbers, and some way forward.

Let us then agree that the extremely high rate of children in poverty limits their life chances, and therefore higher aspirations for our country. If children have lower IQ, are less healthy, and have less chance or interest in academic achievement, then our world marketplace competition is depressed. Market leadership will be based on innovation and productivity, so we need to consider all the children of our nation, not just our own. However, unless families care for their own children *first*, we will have an undoable project on our hands.

Lower IQ

Clinton points out a study that shows that poor babies given cognitive stimulation (by professionals) had their IQs raised to 100, the set average. This is dramatic – and realistic. Every one of us could have smarter kids, if we worked on it. Some families work on it a lot. These are families that started out with smart parents, whose money and position in society came from academic achievement, who have two parents working on it, and who are probably having great results, barring health problems, business failure, or local economic collapse. The study, however, was done with poor children. This is why there was such a dramatic increase. Let me give you some anecdotes so you can see what we are talking about.

I met a family at a church camping trip that had two children of their own and a couple they were fostering. There were three boys running around trying to get in a boat, waving a stick and playing with a dog. There was a smaller boy clinging to the mother. It was hard to tell how old he was. He looked like maybe three, but he was the size of maybe 14 months. He clung to the mother – obviously not his mother, given the dramatic difference in skin color.

I stopped and chatted, since the parents were having coffee and the last bit of breakfast, obviously relaxed as the older boys were playing within jumping distance. They explained their family situation – why the two colors. "This is Bowling Ball," the mother said. I must have looked shocked. Well, we started calling him that because, when he came to us, he had the IQ of a bowling ball. He acted like a bowling ball. I guess nobody ever did anything with him. Now, he will say a few words, feed himself, and all. He has come a l-o-o-n-n-g-g way."

Later that night around the campfire, she told me she had decided maybe it wasn't very good to call the boy "Bowling Ball" anymore. I agreed.

Another time, I was waiting for my eyeglasses to be fixed when a young mother, her immigrant father and her baby came in. They sat beside me, and must have been waiting for some glasses too. I noticed that the girl handed the baby a bottle in the stroller and propped it up. I asked if I could feed the baby the bottle. Given permission, I picked up the baby, held it with the head on the left side resting on my upper arm, put the bottle in the baby's mouth, looked in his eyes and started talking to him. Wow, he liked this! His expressionless face turned to a smile.

"See, this is the way to hold the baby when you feed him. You know, in daycares, it is illegal to give babies propped up bottles."

"Really? I never hold him."

"Oh, my, it is very important to hold a baby – and to talk to him."

"He can't understand. He can't talk."

"He does know if you are talking to him. See him smile at me?"

"How old is he?"

"Nine months."

"Really? He is about the size of a four-month old."

"I know. He is small."

"He is small because he is not happy. He is not happy because he doesn't know you love him. You should hold him and talk to him."

When my glasses came, she was holding the baby, talking to him, and he was really smiling and laughing.

You may know of children warehoused in eastern European orphanages. They didn't grow. Some died. Some who are adopted still have attachment and mental problems because of what they went through. Health and IQ are dramatically affected by the kind of cognitive, emotional, maybe even spiritual stimulation that the baby is given.

Poverty can lower IQ; lower IQs can increase poverty. Therefore, it is a reasonable problem for those who make policy to address. If you are a citizen, this means you. If you are a parent, it is your first priority.

Academic Achievement

Today, there is a good deal of discussion about increasing academic achievement, unfortunately much of it deceptive; but, at least, policy-makers are finally concerned. We all should be, because we have the lowest K-12 academic achievement in the industrialized world, and indeed fall behind many developing nations. I trust that is is evident that poor children have lower achievement on average, and that a nation with low academic achievement will fare poorly in the world marketplace.

The good news on the educational front is that the United States has traditionally led the world in graduate education. It is for this reason that computers and iPhones and such things are designed in the United States, even though often they may be built elsewhere; so, they have a growing middle-class while ours is declining. On the other hand, it has been decades that foreign students have over-represented in science, technology and math fields. At some point, other nations will have graduate schools that compete with ours. At some point, those graduates will want to live at home. Then, we are in trouble.

Our recent efforts to increase STEM (science, technology engineering and math) achievement have made some limited progress. It is limited because our early math teaching is about as bad as it possibly can be. Our general efforts to increase rigor have had some limited improvement for the worst schools (where they were typically graduating illiterates); but, overall, the achievement is down, contrary to reports. College board scores were re-centered – downward. Lots of tests do not mean more rigor; they do mean less instructional time. James Popham, consultant for test construction, in his *The Truth about Testing* (2003), compellingly shows the cycle of making easy tests so districts look good, forcing teachers to teach down to them, reducing morale about students, and then responding with even easier tests – all the while making parents happy with apparently good scores.

We are in serious trouble. In public education, the expenditure per student is greater than all but the most expensive private schools. In public education, we are in debt. We are greatly in debt in most states and at the national level. We cannot reasonably increase expenditures in public education.

Fortunately, James Coleman, the foremost sociologist of education, in his 1986 study, showed that, even greater than family background and income, the expectations of the adults around a student is the biggest predictor for success. Therefore, we could simply change our expectations. We could be a "stand-and-deliver nation." Unfortunately, our nation has become very anti-intellectual. Being smart is bad. Education is bad. If teachers are not not well paid and treated, consider the majority of college instructors. Most adjuncts are educated like doctors and paid worse than janitors. Corporations entering into the field are making matters worse. Trends are grim, because we do not care about education.

Health

Clinton brings up health concerns for children, but she addresses *only* vaccinations! Today, focusing on vaccinations as the number one answer to improving children's health looks very curious indeed. More affluent parents are staying away from vaccinations as the most popular suspect for the terrible, life debilitating disorder of autism. Diseases like chicken pox have such small statistics in this country that vaccinations do not seem worth the risk. The fact that governments are spending extra money and effort on advertising, recommending and even requiring new vaccinations is met with increasing and well-earned skepticism. It is assumed that the drug companies' profit motive is behind the government's "concern." It is very concerning that, given abundant anecdotal evidence and years of scientific, peer-reviewed studies that suggest toxicity is the culprit, governments are stonewalling against more safety testing and occasionally persecuting reputable, world-class researchers. Worse, there are billboards in the poor part of town picturing a baby saying, "No shots; no kisses;" they are not winning hearts.

We do have health problems in our population as never before. Beside the health problems that have dogged the poor, we have new concerns, the most pressing of which ironically center on vaccinations.

We have a serious pandemic in the "autism spectrum disorder." Even allowing for category shifts, we have a pandemic increase. Current levels alone break our public education system. The latest figures that the CDC published say among 8-year-olds that one in 54 boys and 1 in 252 girls are affected. The CDC holds that vaccines are not related and that new safety studies have been done on eight vaccines, but they have not said if there have been studies on combinations, which was what was at issue.

Further, there are numerous cases of contraction rates falling after immunizations were stopped.

Of course, there is always some risk involved in vaccinating, such as in contracting meningitis – of which each of us is informed and given knowledge about what to look for, right? What is surprising is that there have been some reported cases of epidemics having been started by the immunization campaigns (http://www.vaccineriskawareness.com/The-Herd-Immunity-Theory-Treating-Our-Children-Like-Cattle), yet there continues to be not only claims of "we-know-nothing" but also stepped-up expenditures to push vaccines.

Furthermore, separate from the toxicity issues, concerns about vaccines creating strokes in infants has been demonstrated by Dr. Andrew Moulden from Canada. The vaccine particles are too big for babies' small capillaries, thus causing stroke. No one looks for strokes in babies, of course, but Moulden's before-and-after pictures of babies' faces are compelling.

It is beyond the scope of this work to sort out these claims. Let's just notice that today we cannot answer the concern about children's health with a blithe suggestion about government-enforced vaccinations! Would Mrs. Clinton like to have her daughter's body invaded by a bureaucracy, over her own opinions and her doctor's research, in a way that might truly wreck her life? Of course she wouldn't. Therefore, it is not good policy for anyone else.

An even more generalized threat is the everyday germ. Every child is exposed to cold and flu germs, but of course a great deal more if they are in group care or school. There is alarm now in medical and public health literature about the spread of contagious disease in daycares. It is well established that children who are sick a lot not only miss time in which they could be learning, but also are spending their energy getting well instead of growing and learning. Indeed, increased days of sickness may mean a drag on IQ!

Beyond exposure to toxins and exposure to germs, there is the even more general problem of poor nutrition. While feeding children is somewhat addressed by governmental policy, but also greatly exacerbated by what is available in schools and what is demanded for licensed childcare centers; while parents in some states have ousted commercial fast food and soda pop from some K-12 schools, the average school lunch is not very nutritious. Often, these lunches are unduly small, as well. The excess from farm subsidies, such as hormone-laced milk and highly colored cheese, are siphoned to the schools, leading one food activist to claim that we are using our public school children for garbage disposals. Often, breakfasts are laced with sugar and even red dye! Early childhood centers are required to push standard milk on all students. Families must provide a doctor's note if they wish to – or need to – provide different or better food for their children. Notice, please, that doctors typically do not study nutrition; they probably know less than the average devoted middle class mother. The poor single mother, of course, cannot fight the bureaucracy and must succumb to government's enforcement of food quality that a richer woman would not tolerate. Numerous charts extolling vegetables' virtues cannot topple government coercion coupled with big business advertisement. Given the agreed upon impact of nutrition upon IQ and achievement, and given that the government plays such a large part in food, it is truly amazing that neither Clinton's book then nor the general public now are adequately addressing this issue.

More Contributive To Society

While Clinton does not directly address the lack of morals, ethics and altruism as one of her major concerns, I would like to add this to the short list of problems. Employers today are complaining about their recent graduate new hires lacking self-application, work ethic and social skills. None of this is inculcated in our educational system because of the No Child Left Behind program. While it was intended to increase rigor and to help those children falling between the cracks, what really happened was that teachers were not permitted to fail students. When failing was not an option, and teaching was aimed as low as possible, all students were cultured in laziness.

Even previous to NCLB, it has been the consensus of our society that we could not teach morals and ethics in public schools because religion would be too divisive or coercive. (Notice the assumption in this argument that morals are rooted in a religion.) In a time when society's morals were changing and most mothers were employed, this meant the most important part of socialization and teaching – character formation – was entirely neglected.

Clearly today, too many of our society are "entitled," still more are self-centered, and very few live to serve. Indeed, in colleges, altruism is often taught to be non-existent or considered to be a mental illness! This must change. If the human character were reformed – or resurrected – then our problems of poverty, violence, and other intractable economic and social problems would soon be solved. What we teach, or choose not to teach our children, relates to how they will grow up and contribute to, or take from, society.

Conclusion To Introduction

It is time we faced our problems. Yes, we should accept Hilary Clinton's invitation to dialog on the well-being of our children. We must not wave away the discussion because her solutions are horribly wrong. Further, we cannot, simply because we wish to help the poor and believe in early childhood education, fail to really consider the complexity of the problem and the likely result of our favored policy. Rather than banal mothering advice and winsome stories about my family, a serious consideration of the lack of progress we have with existing policies and possible untried solutions are needed. So, in Chapter 2, let's consider Clinton's assumptions; and in Chapter 3, let's ask what kind of a village we want and what are likely ways to create it. Then let us consider some problems and promises of existing situations, government programs (Chapter 4), then the need for saying "no" in our overly sexualized culture (Chapter 5), as well as consider the impact of the self-esteem movement in education (Chapter 6), and then discover what kind of education regularly outperforms in Chapter 7. Finally, in Chapter 8, let's consider some ideas for transformation.

Chapter Two

The Government is not a Village

In her book, *It Takes a Village*, Hilary Clinton shares the very real concerns of a mother, a lawyer and a Democrat. This is, of course, entirely reasonable for Hillary Clinton of the 1990s. At the time, I would have agreed with most of her suggestions. Well, really they are arguments. We suspect we have a political agenda that is decorated by personal stories. Surely that is entirely forgivable. However, from the vantage point of today, the implication that government should intervene in early childhood seems naive, if not dangerous, because the government is not a village.

The work was most criticized on the basis that children need parents more than government policies. To her credit, Clinton does say clearly early on that children need parents. On the other hand, it is true that parents are best supported by extended family and "the village." She mentions small towns of yesteryear. I do think many people are trying to replace the extended family and tribe. Clinton jumps very quickly, however, to national governmental policy. To jump so quickly and directly to government intervention would be an error. To be fair, she does mention several salutary non-profit programs, which we should notice. We also need to consider more carefully what all the possibilities are. Before we pick the government option, we must carefully assess both the reasonable potential and the likely harm.

Clinton valiantly fought for the good of children, first as a lawyer in Arkansas, and then as governor's wife, and later as First Lady. It is no wonder or fault that she might write on behalf of policy aimed at improving the lives of children. There is a giant gap, however, between a mother's concern and the immediate leap to government policy.

Gaps in Understanding

Before considering these gaps, I would like to consider the gap in understanding on the issue between the conservatives and the liberals.

Conservatives wave away the entire discussion with, "No! It takes parents!" Well, of course Clinton clearly said:

> Parents bear the first and primary responsibility for their sons and daughters – to feed them, to sing them to sleep, to teach them to ride a bike, to encourage their talents, to help them develop spiritual lives, to make countless daily decisions that determine whom they have the potential to become (p.11).

Small nods like this, and throughout the book in her anecdotes about her rearing and her parenting, show that she clearly assumed, like we all do, that optimally parents take the primary role as caregivers and teachers to their children. Thus, it is an unfair criticism, or shallow, or suspicious to counter with, "It takes parents." What Clinton overtly argues in the book is that parents are not enough – or we cannot rely on parents only – because there are too many children without functional parents. There is a need for charity and thus policy.

Unfortunately, the Democrats, and indeed I think Clinton herself, have failed to understand the philosophical grounding or the kernel of truth in the retort. It does take parents. Government certainly, and to some extent any group or program, cannot replace parents. Thus, the best policy would be to build parents. Unfortunately, government policies tend to do the reverse, detracting from parents.

Addressing the problems she suggests, such as early childhood education through government intervention, will fall short at best and likely make the problems worse. This argument has added weight since fifteen years hence, after many programs, policies and government intervention, particularly in education. The problems are even worse now. Divorce is up, child poverty is up, violence in school is way up, and real academic achievement is down. Thus, we certainly do not need more of what has not worked.

Unfortunately, the conservatives tend not to see much beyond their own comfortable hearth. To liberals, they appear not to take seriously their responsibility for the good of the whole. Yes, we need personal responsibility; but, yes, we also need civic responsibility. Clinton is right that the father's wage-earning capacity hinges today largely on the economy, and the father alone cannot make the streets safe. Expectations about marriage and divorce are larger than the couple alone. There is, indeed, a larger context. It does not help the discussion when those on the right merely dismiss the concerns of the left.

The left appears to have a good grasp of the social problems. Please notice, however, the logic slip that assuming the need for charity means a need for governmental policy. Notice an even worse logical slip: that policies originally meant as charitable for the poor should be enforced on all but the wealthy. The right points out that the left's solutions are not working; worse, they could slide quickly into dictatorial communism. By bread and circuses, the peons may be amused, while the elite gather more control. Thus, the republic is lost. Civic duty primarily consists of eternal vigilance for freedom; monetary equality is of little worth compared to freedom, even if it weren't entirely chimerical.

Liberals might appeal to conservatives to engage in working on the problem of the well-being of children by pointing out that a higher IQ and better academic performance will permit a better business climate. Conservatives might better show how their own policies won't slide into dictatorial fascism. Anyone interested in self-governance or the good of our country should be interested in higher academic achievement. The first law that encouraged a public school was called the "Old Deluder Satan Act," because it was thought that we should ensure that all children in society could read the Bible and the laws so that they could compare them and "watchdog" the government. Surely, there is a way to do that. First, we must pull ourselves out of the mire of deadlock between "liberals" and "conservatives," and then bridge the gaps. Let's earn a better outcome for our children and a future for our society.

Gaps

Let us consider, then, some of these gaps between genuine concern for children's well-being. Let's look at this leap to solve it by government intervention: (1) there is a gap between what parents can do and what governments can do; (2) there is a gap between what parents do and what needs to be done; (3) there is a gap beyond what the government has done and what we would like to have seen; and (4) there is a gap beyond what needs to be done and what it is possible for a government to do by itself. After we discuss these gaps, let us ask how these gaps may be filled. We will ask what kind of village we may need for child welfare in a later chapter.

(1) Gap between Parents' and Governments' Abilities

There is a gap between what parents can do and what governments can do. Undeniably, parents, as the first caregivers, are highly influential to the child. Because of this, they are indispensable to society. For instance, it has been said that the mother is the first bulwark against crime. There could never be enough police in a society unless most of the citizens wanted to obey the law most of the time. They do so because, when they were tots, their mother told them, "Don't hit," and the like. Parents are the first socializers, the ones who form behavior. Neither governments nor businesses can do this. They cannot because they do not intend to. They cannot because they depend upon paid labor – who will go home, quit, and be promoted. They cannot because they are not biologically, spiritually, fundamentally, to the root of their being attached to the child. Only parents, not organizations, can love with parental love.

Organizations are not capable of love. Many *people* are not capable of the kind of self-giving love required to be a good parent.

Notice government orphanages of eastern Europe. Eastern Europeans are not monsters. It is simply that governments cannot be parents. Indeed, quite unfortunately, we have had tragic orphanages here too. It is possible that an organization can do better or less well. It is possible that employees can be surrogate parents for a time. Eventually their boss will intervene, the budget will be cut, or they will move on in order to provide for their own family. Institutions cannot equal the love, the self-giving, the heartstrings of parents.

Similarly, we might compare how well public school students are socialized (meaning taught how to behave as competent adults in their society) with children who are home-educated. Which student knows manners, can manage themselves, and can talk with adults most competently? There is no contest at all. One might think that the government, hiring professional educators, could teach manners – or at least academics. Anyone who has seen the statistics knows that on average the home-educated students handily outperform. Anyone who has seen many home-educated children also knows that they are much more socially competent in the adult world. Of course, there are variations – in both camps. However, contrary to common prejudice, it is rather intuitive that the child who gets more attention from adults and socializes with handpicked peers is likely to be better socialized than the child who is herded with many his age, kept quiet and still, and given only a few minutes a day of adult attention.

There is a gap between what government can do and what only parents can do. Government cannot rear children because bureaucracies certainly do not have love. We might quixotically hope that we could make bureaucracies have wisdom or overcome their innate tendency to take care of and expand their own power, but we could never hope to have a bureaucracy be loving.

(2) Gap Between What Parents Are Doing and What Must be Done

However, it must also be admitted that there is a gap between what parents are actually doing currently and what needs to be done. Some parents are not able to adequately fill the parental role. For instance, some young mothers are not able to make enough money to take care of their children. Similarly, it is possible for the government to provide food enough for everyone, and government and others do provide much food, but some children still go hungry. Further, although how enforcement is conducted matters, still parents are not adequately socializing their children to stay out of gangs and out of crime. There has always been some difference in outcome based on the ability and dedication of parents.

Many children have benefited from what others in the community have done to make up for the deficiencies in their parents' ability. Many have cited the coach's attention, the double duty of a grandparent, or the graciousness of an aunt or uncle. Some think fondly of a pastor or Sunday School teacher. A few have gratefully cited what a foster parent or orphanage has done.

Today, probably most families are hard-pressed to cover all the duties they are expected to cover. At one time, most families had father pontificating at the dinner table and mother helping with the homework; while, today, probably most eat separately on the run. Most families purchased music lessons and brought their children to Sunday School (or Hebrew School); but, today, a greater proportion feel that they cannot afford lessons and do not have the money to fit in some organized group. Most schools had PTAs (Parent Teacher Associations) that not only raised money for projects but also remonstrated with the administration when things were not right. They depended, however, on mothers who worked in the home. Today, mothers and grandmothers more typically are employed. Most cities had a ministerial alliance that "bully-pulpited" as well as had encouraging words with city officials when necessary. Increasingly, administrators have found a way to co-opt PTAs, and ministerial alliances have been marginalized. More hours at work, more time at the gym, more time on electronic media, and in some home more pressure of extracurricular activities around achievement, means less time interacting with children and less time in religious or civic engagement or for those children.

(3) Gap Between What Government Has Done and Was Asked to Do

Not surprisingly, then, there is a gap beyond what the government has done and what we would like to have seen. We have called for increased rigor in our education system. Although the scores appear to have gone up, the real expectations for the students have gone down. Although students, parents and some politicians may not know it, (1) tests are constructed to be as easy as possible in order to make districts look good; (2) the system is planned for incremental gains rather than maximum quick gains; and (3) teaching to the tests violates the sampling philosophy behind tests. The SAT had to be re-centered downward. College professors have to aim lower every few years. James Popham, consultant who built many of those tests has "spilled the beans" in his 2003 book, *The Truth About Testing.* Government schools are falling even further behind.

One underlying reason for school failure is poverty. The government has vigorously addressed poverty. The Lyndon Johnson War on Poverty had dramatic effect, greatly reducing the numbers in poverty at the time. The Clinton administration worked to reduce welfare rolls and reduce the federal deficit by helping recipients transition to work. Yet, we still see generational welfare. It was Barbara Jordan, an African-American Democrat from Houston, who pronounced at a Democratic convention that we must work against an entitlement mentality. Yet, it has increased!

One root problem of having so many young children in dire circumstances is the high rate of young, unwed pregnancies. Clinton cites it as 30% in her book. Today, the percentage of children born without a father in the home (officially) is 35.7! George W. Bush's administration sought to encourage marriage, and hired some counselors to encourage young people applying for welfare or having a baby between them to marry. Yet, few did, and the tide of opinion that it is acceptable to have children out of wedlock rises. The percentage of young women who think that having a child out of wedlock is fine is dramatically up. Further, deviant sexual practices are encouraged.

There is some evidence that unintended pregnancies now are down except for the poorer women. There is evidence that a percentage of these pregnancies being aborted is down (http://www.guttmacher.org/pubs/FB-Unintended-Pregnancy-US.html#15). There is further evidence that, when contraception is paid for by the government, there is a savings of other government expenditures for abortions or births (Gold RB et al., Next Steps for America's Family Planning Program: Leveraging the Potential of Medicaid and Title X in an Evolving Health Care System, New York: Guttmacher Institute, 2009). Yet, we continue to have a very high rate, no good dialog, and no viable way forward.

Several administrations have promised educational reform, and yet achievement continues to tank (although, often with parents thinking that rigor has actually increased due to deceptive statistics and rhetoric). Barak Obama campaigned with the promise to dismantle No Child Left Behind and see the continuing achievement gap by ethnicity as this decades civil rights issue; but, in office, he has said he did not intend to dismantle high-stakes testing, and the gap continues. In the last school board meeting here, the president of the school board seriously asked what increased rigor meant. In discussion, it was agreed to discover what people meant when they asked for increased rigor in education.

Remembering Paul Tsongas (D), who said, "If anyone thinks the words government and efficiency belong in the same sentence, we have counseling available" (Kramer, Time, March 2, 1992), it is probably not hard to find instances where the government has failed to meet its goals in terms of changing itself, let alone society. Academic performance, poverty and underlying family inability, all of which the government appears to be addressing, nevertheless has continued to dive to lower levels.

(4) Gap Between Desirable Outcome and What Government Can Do

There is a gap beyond what it is possible for a government to do by itself. Government cannot, and should not, attempt to reach everywhere. There is a considerable gap between what needs to be done in society that government is trying to cover and has not been able to. There is a gap beyond what parents do that government can't reach and no one else is, although someone could.

Someone needs to rear parents and support them with good peer pressure. Someone needs to be the extended family. Sometimes, some people may need to be a substitute family. Someone does need to be employer and mentor for dads and some mothers. Someone needs to help with education; with prevention, wellness and healing, information delivery, and fine culture/fun.

Some of these things only "the village" can do. Government, business, non-profits, churches and religious organizations, voluntary associations, and every citizen needs to be part of this.

We have to mobilize ourselves, help others mobilize, and watchdog those inappropriately mobilized. Everyone needs to help with making this a livable culture.

You may be asking, how realistic is this? Who could make this happen? It may seem easier to foist a task off onto the government; but, after all, who is the government? Is it us? Or is it them? Either way you answer, you see it is high time to wake up, get up, get going, get effective, and get free.

Okay, so how might freedom be engendered, rather than a food fight? By consensus values! This is what the founders of our country meant when they said that only a moral and religious people could be governed democratically.

> [V]irtue or morality is a necessary spring of popular government.   George Washington

> [I]t is religion and morality alone which can establish the principles upon which freedom can securely stand. The only foundation of a free constitution is pure virtue.   John Adams

> Only a virtuous people are capable of freedom. As nations become more corrupt and vicious, they have more need of masters.   Benjamin Franklin

> No government can continue good but under the control of the people; and . . . . their minds are to be informed by education what is right and what wrong; to be encouraged in habits of virtue and to be deterred from those of vice . . . . These are the inculcations necessary to render the people a sure basis for the structure and order of government.
>   Thomas Jefferson

> It is in the manners and spirit of a people which preserve a republic in vigour. . . . degeneracy in

these is a canker which soon eats into the heart of its laws and constitution.　　　Thomas Jefferson

The institution of delegated power implies that there is a portion of virtue and honor among mankind which may be a reasonable foundation of confidence.　　　Alexander Hamilton

To suppose that any form of government will secure liberty or happiness without any virtue in the people is a chimerical idea.　　James Madison

. . . Virtue, morality, and religion. This is the armor, my friend, and this alone that renders us invincible. These are the tactics we should study. If we lose these, we are conquered, fallen indeed . . . so long as our manners and principles remain sound, there is no danger.　　　Patrick Henry

These men knew very well that people fought over various versions of their religion; but, at the end of the day, they knew that, without morality *grounded in religion,* society was not possible. There was some consensus about morality in their society, and that it was for better, rather than worse, behavior.

Who Can Fill in the Gaps?

Clearly parents are necessary. But, better parents would be better. Who in society is tasked and capable, at least potentially so, to instruct people in how to marry, how to parent, and how to be self-giving? Clearly, families are helpful. Better families; more prosperous, more wise, more giving would be better. Who in society is tasked, capable and interested in helping families arrive at this aim? What should be made of the huge percentage of young children who are not in intact families? Will we envision a sea change of extended families taking on the task of covering single mothers?

Certainly, media, education, government and business alike could be part of this effort to support families in order to be a child-friendly culture, in order to raise IQ, academic achievement, well-being and moral character. We do want this; we simply have not had the aim clearly in our sights. Who could make the village better?

How might the government be part of this? It is unlikely that the government will any time soon adopt the place of moral teacher, since secularism is currently the popular viewpoint. If it were to do so, while being secular, it might look scarily like either fascism or communism. Surely we would not want to impose this, and indeed may want to dismantle as much as we already have. However, the government might encourage private efforts to teach morality, altruism and the pursuit of excellence. It could at least be more careful to refrain from denigrating, squelching and even persecuting those who are doing so.

Then First Lady Clinton indeed has done us a service in inviting us into a dialog concerning the well-being of children. Let this be a real, intelligent and honest discussion. Let us refrain from being sucked into the L/R push-me/pull-you 30-second soundbite nonsense that continually distracts us while picking our pocket. Children are too important to use as playthings! We need at once to be open to more creative, innovative ideas, *and to* stop rejecting those old answers that always worked and demonstrably work for others.

Works Cited

"QUOTES ON LIBERTY AND VIRTUE" Compiled & ed. by J. David Gowdy. http://www.liberty1.org/virtue.htm

CAN YOU HELP GET THE WORD OUT?

Tell 5 friends about this book, about the ideas to improve this nation, and tell them buy this book. Then get: a pin that says "The Government is not a Village" as a thank you gift. Just give proof you did this (photocopy your letters or copy your emails) and send us your land address. Write me at P.O. Box 971 Cedar Park Texas 78630 or sharon@thegovernmentisnotavillage.com (through 2015)

Chapter Three

What Kind of Village?

We are agreed, then, that parents have the primary duty for children. We are also agreed that surrounding adults are important in providing an environment tending to well-being. Thus, by extension, we must be agreed that we all hold some private duties and civic responsibility, though we must consider what those entail. Once having done that, we might take the question of what role the government might play in children's well-being.

Parents

It is agreed that parents are the first and most important part of the picture of a happy world for children. It is also agreed that not all do their job. How might we inspire parents to aspire to being great parents? If you were talking to a young couple, what sort of message would you give them? If you could build society, how would you construct it so that parents would be motivated? What sort of moral tutor might be employed?

What have been the best mechanisms? Religion. Public opinion, based on religion. Culture, based on morality, based on religion. This has been true in traditional and modern societies. If government were to take on that moral function or employ religion, however, it would be tyrannical. It would be ineffective to the degree it was tyrannical. Either it would be monolithically and ineptly enforced and hurtful, or it would be largely rebelled against at least by being ignored. Just as if you were to attempt to enforce your view on a young couple, government enforcement works only to a limited extent. We tried this in European culture, and discarded it with the Edict of Nantes. Asian cultures have tried other permutations, none of which now exist. Governments can enforce religion, or irreligion, but will never see as great a result as free religion has. When religion was free, it seemed to be the strongest. Many governments have seen a good result by promoting a workable variety. The idea of a government countering traditional values, and religion with it, has never seen a good result. Freely chosen religion is what best molds behavior to the salutary.

What kind of religion, then, best encourages parenting? Perhaps many would like to enter into this contest, and certainly many teach respect to parents. Which teaches respect for children? Which most centrally ensconces the duty of parents?

The Judeo-Christian religion clearly does so. Abraham was chosen because he would "command" his children (as the King James Version renders it.)

> For I [G-d] know [Abraham] him, that will command his children and his household after him, and they shall keep the way of the LORD, to do justice and judgment; that the LORD may bring upon Abraham that which he hath spoken of him. Genesis 18:19 KJV

> 19 For I have chosen him, so that he will direct his children and his household after him to keep the way of the Lord by doing what is right and just, so that the Lord will bring about for Abraham what he has promised him." NIV

The duty of parents to ALWAYS teach their children is put next to the Sh'ma, the central tenant of monotheism, in Deuteronomy 6.

> 3 Hear therefore, O Israel, and observe to do *it;* that it may be well with thee, and that ye may increase mightily, as the LORD God of thy fathers

hath promised thee, in the land that floweth with milk and honey.

4 Hear, O Israel: The LORD our God *is* one LORD:

5 And thou shalt love the LORD thy God with all thine heart, and with all thy soul, and with all thy might.

6 And these words, which I command thee this day, shall be in thine heart:

7 And thou shalt teach them diligently unto thy children, and shalt talk of them when thou sittest in thine house, and when thou walkest by the way, and when thou liest down, and when thou risest up.

8 And thou shalt bind them for a sign upon thine hand, and they shall be as frontlets between thine eyes.

9 And thou shalt write them upon the posts of thy house, and on thy gates.

Central to both Jewish and Christian faith, parents are tasked with teaching their children, always and particularly, about the spiritual/ethical. We certainly are not looking for a religion that would posit children and wives as chattel and permit abuse of either. Hinduism and Buddhism certainly teach respect of parents, but have little in the way of tasking parents with duties. Native/earth-based religions typically encourage respect for parents and grandparents, but are spotty in their expectations of parents; some are harsh, others lenient, and there is no universal dictum about teaching; however, much learning from elders is central. Similarly, Sikhism, while embracing householding and highly valuing education culturally, does not have central dictums around teaching children. It is the Judeo-Christian religion, then, that has the most clear and the most beneficial vision and rule for teaching and positively guiding children.

One thing we might be alerted to by an excursus to other religions is how much the extended family is both valued and tasked with helping. Native American religions and Hindu culture both hold the expectation that children whose parents cannot care for them are to be cared for by the extended family. Although this has not been the case recently in Western culture (since the Industrial Revolution or since socialism?) it was often the case previously. The tribal culture of ancient Israel may suggest that such was originally the expectation. Second Timothy does task adult children (and the church) with helping widows.

Further, contrary to the warped picture of Biblical Christians as angry abusers, love and grace is integrally wrapped up in this very command – as well as the warp and woof of the rest of both traditions. There is a reason why Jews' most holy books are called the Torah, the Law: because the ethical imperative was central. Christians would use the term "right relationships" with both God and humans in this context. (Some Christians would suggest that there are two categories of law, the ethical law and the ceremonial law; however, it is all about right relationships.) What many Christians do not realize, as they are informed by the Apostle Paul's polemic against the *Judiaizers in the Gentile church* rather than against Judaism itself, is that grace is also central to the Hebrew religion. The Torah was a *gift* from God. God made a covenant with Israel, not because of their righteousness but because of His own nature of love and grace. Therefore, both groups base their central ethics on God's love, grace and faithfulness/*hesed*. *Thus,* in the command to teach one's children, to direct them, is inherently the command to do so in love.

The admonition to teach one's children rather than neglect them continues through the history of Israel. Famous passages in Proverbs, attributed to Solomon, follow:

> Foolishness *is* bound in the heart of a child; *but* the rod of correction shall drive it far from him. Proverbs 22:15 KJV

> Withhold not correction from the child: for *if* thou beatest him with the rod, he shall not die. Proverbs 23:13 KVJ

> The rod and reproof give wisdom: but a child left *to himself* bringeth his mother to shame. Proverbs 29:15 KJV

In an attempt to see what the ancient Hebrews had in mind, as opposed to our Elizabethan ancestors, let's consult some newer translations.

> Proverbs 23:13 Withhold not *musar* (correction) from the *na'ar* (child), for if thou spank him with the *shevet*, he shall not die. Mishle

> 13 Withhold not discipline from the child; for if you strike and punish him with the [reedlike] rod, he will not die. Amplified

> 13 Don't hesitate to discipline children. A good spanking won't kill them. Good News Translation

> 13 Don't fail to correct your children. You won't kill them by being firm. Contemporary English Version

> 13-14 Don't be afraid to correct your young ones; a spanking won't kill them. A good spanking, in fact, might save them from something worse than death. Message

While these are despised today as promoting abuse, I would submit that we see the insanity of that position with today's large mass of our youth who have been neglected; not taught self-restraint, ethics, or altruism; who think the world owes them an entertainment. We have made, by our policies, the entitlement generation. Entitlement seems to have grown so much that some people have different, even opposite, definitions. I mean by "entitlement" that we have cultivated an expectation that goods and services come as a matter of due course or "rights" rather than from work, reciprocity or charity. This attitude is one of demanding things, with no moral basis to do so, while at the same time not rendering what is due. It is an attitude that sees oneself as the center of the universe. This is predictable in a toddler, but evidences lack of teaching from anyone older. The lack of moral teaching is neglect, a kind of abuse.

The prophets also include a statement about the parental relationship; and while it is a statement about the end times, it still applies to parents.

> Behold, I will send you Elijah the prophet before the coming of the great and dreadful day of the LORD:
> 6 And he shall turn the heart of the fathers to the children, and the heart of the children to their fathers, lest I come and smite the earth with a curse. Malachi 4: 4&5 KJV

Indeed, it may be a sign of the times that we need to write a patient teaching on how to inspire parents to love their children! And do so wisely.

Here are the passages from the New Testament.

> And, ye fathers, provoke not your children to wrath: but bring them up in the nurture and admonition of the Lord. Ephesians 6:4 KJV

> Fathers, provoke not your children *to anger,* lest they be discouraged. Colossians 3:21 KJV

Notice the repetition in the text that seems to be unquoted, even unknown, today by detractors. Let's see these verses in other translations. Notice the point about everything being wrapped in love.

Ephesians 6: 4

4 Fathers, do not exasperate your children; instead, bring them up in the training and instruction of the Lord. NIV

4 Fathers, do not irritate and provoke your children to anger [do not exasperate them to resentment], but rear them [tenderly] in the training and discipline and the counsel and admonition of the Lord. Amplified

4 Fathers, don't irritate your children and make them resentful; instead, raise them with the Lord's kind of discipline and guidance. Complete Jewish Bible

4 Fathers, don't make your children angry, but raise them with the kind of teaching and training you learn from the Lord. Easy to Read Version

4 Fathers, don't exasperate your children by coming down hard on them. Take them by the hand and lead them in the way of the Master. Message

Colossians 3:21

21 Fathers, do not provoke or irritate or fret your children [do not be hard on them or harass them], lest they become discouraged and sullen and morose and feel inferior and frustrated. [Do not break their spirit.] Amplified

21 Fathers [or Parents; Heb. 11:23], do not nag [aggravate; exasperate; provoke] your children [Eph. 6:4]. If you are too hard to please, they may want to stop trying [become discouraged; lose heart]. Expanded Bible

21 Fathers, don't over-correct your children, or they will grow up feeling inferior and frustrated. Phillips

21 Parents, don't come down too hard on your children or you'll crush their spirits. Message

21 Fathers, do not embitter your children, or they will become discouraged. New International Version

21 Fathers, do not make your children angry. They might stop trying to do right. Worldwide English

21 The fathers! Vex not your children, lest they be discouraged. Young's Literal Translation

So, here we have a reasonable assessment of what the Judeo-Christian tradition teaches parents to do. It fits with our need for moral training that enforces boundaries and does so with wisdom, grace and love. It is precisely the kind of moral admonition that will work to encourage better parenting.

Would any religion suffice? No. Any religion that teaches selfishness would not suffice. Any religion that is centered on hate or would sacrifice children for adult ends would not suffice. What would be the characteristics of a religion that would best cultivate parents and society? A religion centered on love, but not without strong ethical boundaries. Ideally, we need a religion whose God is an example of self-giving love. Good parents must be self-giving, so this would be the best encouragement.

What Kind of Private Duty Should We Encourage for all?

How might we best cultivate a healthy village? We want a village where people are industrious, take care of themselves and their family, and then have enough to give away to those in need, and who have the will to do it. Are there any teachings like this?

Yes, many encourage taking care of one's family (although how that is interpreted depends upon the lens of culture). More than one speaks of right ways of proceeding, and thus the need for choosing an ethical lifestyle. I am not aware of any that better encourage industriousness to the point of having largess specifically to contribute to the whole more than the Judeo-Christian tradition.

Although many people have many ideas about what Christianity teaches, let us focus on the unassailable center of the tradition by letting the Bible, the primary witness, speak for itself. By the way, no body of work is better attested to in the history of the world than the New Testament. We can construct the entire New Testament, except for eleven verses, from "the ancient fathers." We know that people gave their lives for the witness it presents. No group of people would do that for a lie. The very words of Jesus have been corroborated by a heretical book, the Gospel of Thomas, preserved by a long-dead opposing group in Egyptian climate. No one can claim, with any reasonable evidence, that we do not, in its words, have the witness of the early church and of Jesus, who claimed to be the Messiah.

The Patriarchs were wealthy.

> Genesis 24:35 The Lord has blessed my master [Abraham] abundantly, and he has become wealthy. He has given him sheep and cattle, silver and gold, male and female servants, and camels and donkeys. NIV

> Genesis 26: 13 The man [Isaac] became rich, and his wealth continued to grow until he became very wealthy. NIV

Clearly, they were portrayed as wealthy. There is no word of reproach about this; but, rather, it is seen as a blessing of God.

> Deut 8:17: And thou say in thine heart, My power and the might of *mine* hand hath gotten me this wealth.
> 18 But thou shalt remember the LORD thy God: for *it*

is he that giveth thee power to get wealth, that he may establish his covenant which he sware unto thy fathers, as *it is* this day. Deuteronomy 8: 17 & 18 KJV

In Deuteronomy 8:18, God gives the power to MAKE wealth, but one is exhorted to remember where that power came from. Deuteronomy portrays Moses' last rehearsal of the law before the people go into the Promised Land. In the 28th chapter of the same book a list of blessings and cursings is recited. Before that, however, there is a direction on how to ritually give thanks for the blessings of good things:

> 11 And thou shalt rejoice in every good *thing* which the LORD thy God hath given unto thee, and unto thine house, thou, and the Levite, and the stranger that *is* among you.
> 12 When thou hast made an end of tithing all the tithes of thine increase the third year, *which is* the year of tithing, and hast given *it* unto the Levite, the stranger, the fatherless, and the widow, that they may eat within thy gates, and be filled;
> 13 Then thou shalt say before the LORD thy God, I have brought away the hallowed things out of *mine* house, and also have given them unto the Levite, and unto the stranger, to the fatherless, and to the widow, according to all thy commandments which thou hast commanded me: I have not transgressed thy commandments, neither have I forgotten *them:*
> 14 I have not eaten thereof in my mourning, neither have I taken away *ought* thereof for *any* unclean *use,* nor given *ought* thereof for the dead: *but* I have hearkened to the voice of the LORD my God, *and* have done according to all that thou hast commanded me.
> 15 Look down from thy holy habitation, from heaven, and bless thy people Israel, and the land which thou hast given us, as thou swarest unto our

fathers, a land that floweth with milk and honey.
Deuteronomy 26:11 KJV

Notice that abundance is to be enjoyed. Next, notice that, once established in the land, people were to set aside a portion to donate to certain categories of people. The Levites were the priestly tribe who were in charge of temple and charity administration; they did draw from this tithe some salary for priestly functions and there was some distribution. There were also portions for strangers, fatherless and widows – or, in other words, the people of that day who were without adequate living: new immigrants, women who had no man to provide for and protect them, and children without fathers. Given that many widows were married to relatives of the deceased, and children were taken in similarly, there was no great proportion of these people. Nevertheless, they were provided for. Further, notice that there is a proscription against using one's material substance for the dead. Of course, Hebrews and Jews today respectfully inter their dead; the proscription is against using this in a ritualistic way that celebrates the macabre and does not help the community. In short, it sounds like making money is valued, and giving some of it away is expected. Further, wealth is to be used for purposes that will be life-giving to the community.

I take Malachi 3:10, which talks about not contributing to the central store, as robbery. God clearly says that, if the Israelites, now back in their land, would contribute to God's house, their houses would be blessed. God will pour out blessings from heaven. In that day, rain was important to the agriculture. Today, many who preach the passage speak of ideas. In any case, there will be so much blessing that it cannot be contained; all nations will call those who serve God blessed.

Certainly, as well as blessings, there are admonitions to do business in an honest way.

Just balances, just weights, a just ephah, and a just hin, shall ye have: I *am* the LORD your God, which brought you out of the land of Egypt. Leviticus 19:36

Thou shalt not have in thy bag divers weights, a great and a small. Deuteronomy 25:13

A just weight and balance *are* the LORD'S: all the weights of the bag *are* his work. Proverbs 16:11

Divers weights, *and* divers measures, both of them *are* alike abomination to the LORD. Proverbs 20:10

Divers weights *are* an abomination unto the LORD; and a false balance *is* not good. Proverbs 20:23

Shall I count *them* pure with the wicked balances, and with the bag of deceitful weights? Micah 6:11 KJV

The admonitions about "weights" demand that measures for trade must be honest and just, not deceptive. Let's look at Proverbs 20:10 in other translations for a better understanding.

10 Diverse weights [one for buying and another for selling] and diverse measures – both of them are exceedingly offensive and abhorrent to the Lord. Amplified

10 A double standard of weights and measures – both are disgusting to the Lord. God's Word Translation

10 The Lord despises every kind of cheating. The Living Bible

10 Switching price tags and padding the expense account are two things God hates. Message

Of course the Torah, wisdom literature like Proverbs and the Prophets, as well as the entire New Testament, are full of directions on how to live an honest and loving life. Bible scholars might sort out *haustafel* (list of how to live at home) from doctrine or history from the rest, but I read it as all entirely useful for instruction on how to live even when written in these other genres. Our question is what kind of private duty must every citizen embrace and live? These are not the only answers from the Bible, but they are what seems important today; they are an adequate representation of how both communities understand that they are instructed. This illustrates the nonsense of what seems to be the viewpoint of our attackers: that God requires killing of those with a separate viewpoint. There were instances, back in the Bronze and Stone Ages, of God's direction in fighting; but these are not general directives for all time, and are not honest representations of general moral directives then, either.

Well, okay, there are severe punishments for those who in their private world significantly detract from the community good. Some people are to be executed. This does include children who are disobedient; but, given that the accusers have to be the parents, I take this to be a very rare situation (large children who are insane and unmanageable, whom even the parents can't see as being contributive). Compared to our society that encourages abortions, enrages parents to readily institutionalize disabled children, takes children away and sometimes unjustly without proper investigations, along with an abundance of medications for teachers' comfort, well, I'm not so sure that our Stone Age predecessors look worse than we do.

What do the (historical Israeli/Judaic) prophets say about religious and civic duty?

> Isaiah 58: religious duty is unimportant without justice and charity.
>
> Employing people justly, moral, and charitable duty comes before religious duties, according to

Isaiah 58:

2 Yet they seek me daily, and delight to know my ways, as a nation that did righteousness, and forsook not the ordinance of their God: they ask of me the ordinances of justice; they take delight in approaching to God.

3 Wherefore have we fasted, *say they,* and thou seest not? W*herefore* have we afflicted our soul, and thou takest no knowledge? Behold, in the day of your fast ye find pleasure, and exact all your labours.

4 Behold, ye fast for strife and debate, and to smite with the fist of wickedness: ye shall not fast as *ye do this* day, to make your voice to be heard on high.

5 Is it such a fast that I have chosen? A day for a man to afflict his soul? I*s it* to bow down his head as a bulrush, and to spread sackcloth and ashes *under him?* Wilt thou call this a fast, and an acceptable day to the LORD?

6 *Is* not this the fast that I have chosen? To loose the bands of wickedness, to undo the heavy burdens, and to let the oppressed go free, and that ye break every yoke?

7 *Is it* not to deal thy bread to the hungry, and that thou bring the poor that are cast out to thy house? When thou seest the naked, that thou cover him; and that thou hide not thyself from thine own flesh?

8 Then shall thy light break forth as the morning, and thine health shall spring forth speedily: and thy righteousness shall go before thee; the glory of the LORD shall be thy rereward.

9 Then shalt thou call, and the LORD shall answer; thou shalt cry, and he shall say, Here I *am.* If thou take away from the midst of thee the yoke,

> the putting forth of the finger, and speaking vanity;
> 10 And *if* thou draw out thy soul to the hungry, and satisfy the afflicted soul; then shall thy light rise in obscurity, and thy darkness *be* as the noonday:
> 11 And the LORD shall guide thee continually, and satisfy thy soul in drought, and make fat thy bones: and thou shalt be like a watered garden, and like a spring of water, whose waters fail not.
> 12 And *they that shall be* of thee shall build the old waste places: thou shalt raise up the foundations of many generations; and thou shalt be called, The repairer of the breach, The restorer of paths to dwell in. Isaiah 58:2-12 KJV

When people wonder why they are not blessed, even though they have gone to some lengths in religion, God tells them that they must treat their employee appropriately.

> 3 Why have we fasted, they say, and You do not see it? Why have we afflicted ourselves, and You take no knowledge [of it]? Behold [O Israel], on the day of your fast [when you should be grieving for your sins], you find profit in your business, and [instead of stopping all work, as the law implies you and your workmen should do] you extort from your hired servants a full amount of labor. Isaiah 58:3. Amplified

Further, they must stop fighting and arguing with each other for God to hear their prayers. Then, they must positively and actively work for the oppressed to not be oppressed but rather free. They must give their own food to the poor and bring them into their own shelter. They must clothe those without clothes. "That thou hide not thyself from thine own flesh" might be read as the Amplified does: And that you hide not yourself from [the needs of] your own flesh and blood?

This may mean anyone of the nation of Israel/Judah, and not members of immediate family. The Complete Jewish Bible renders "from your own kinsmen." Jubilee Bible states "your own brother," which to a Christian with Jesus' words about being a neighbor indicates, "to any fellow human." However, I have always read it to mean that we should realize in this that we ourselves could be in this same position.

Then, if we do that, G-d says that we will receive healing, guidance, protection in difficulty, prosperity, and finally, be called the builder of society. Hmmm. That is what we need today.

Amos is cited as inveighing against social injustice, such a oppressing the poor (Amos 4:1 and 5:10-15). Proverbs urges helping the poor, too, as well as many other directives.

It is not right, however, to skip over something much larger in Law, Wisdom, and Prophets in terms of directives: sexual purity. Reading Amos 5 reminded me. Today, this topic in Scripture is the very most despised by the world, the least preached upon, and the most needed. It is clearly in the Bible that fornication before marriage and adultery after marriage is proscribed. Divorce is not encouraged. Homosexual behavior is clearly forbidden, at least in Romans 1. (Catamitism, sex slavery, is the topic of some of the verses that appear to forbid homosexuality. The Torah seems to overlook lesbianism. So, the complete proscription may be in Romans 1.)

There is no way but admitting that if people behaved in these ways it would be better for children. Hilary Clinton was wise when she said, "Many adults have claimed to have benefited from divorce, but few children have." It is possible, in cases of abuse, but you get the point.

I would admonish pastors to start preaching this topic and to work to help young people form good marriages. I applaud those who have workable real help to keep or re-engage marital partners. I rejoice that now pastors do now preach against domestic abuse.

I do not read anything in the Bible that prevents nonbelievers from having legal rights. However, if homosexuals want to be taken seriously as interested in rights, then they need to (1) ensure that religious families have the right to instruct their children as they see fit about morals, and (2) ensure that others have the right to keep smut out of their own faces. It is not appropriate for heterosexual sex to be put "in someone's face" who doesn't want it, either, but that doesn't typically happen, like homosexuals parading in public and pushing their sexuality in the workplace. I am told that there is a discussion about this in the GLBTQ community; some of them know that they must clean up their image if they wish to promote their cause. It is time the larger discussion broached the topic, too, particularly as relates to children. It is also high time that we talk about the well-being of our children and about our right to practice our religion. It is inappropriate, even atrocious, to suggest that the dominant religion, or any religion which has always taught this to be sin, is now all of a sudden "haters." It is completely inappropriate, as has been done, that training to induce sin should be enforced upon children even without parents' knowledge. It is also inappropriate that parents' concern for the safety of their children be besmirched as discrimination. In a quest for rights, questions of morality and safety must not be shouted down, as they are today.

Amos 5:13 seems appropriate here, talking about a time when the prudent shall have to keep silent. Today, the prudent do keep silent, for fear they will be attacked. However, it is time that we must speak, even sacrificially. It is time we stop thinking about rights for ourselves, and start talking about our duties to children.

Jonah's having to go to Nineveh, home of the archenemy, and saving them by his preaching is an example of overcoming xenophobia. Their listening and repenting of their sin does also.

Micah 6:8 just about sums it up: "He has shewed thee, o man, what is good: and what doth the LORD require of thee but to do justly, and to love mercy and to walk humbly with thy God."

Wow, I have not covered all the laws, for they cover all of life, including sanitation. Imagine that, in the stone age, God's people knew how to avoid infections and how to avoid eating carrion that brought disease! Long before Ignaz Semmelweiss suggested the germ theory, Israelites were washing their hands.

So, what might the New Testament say that is relevant to our ideal village? Once again, the center is relation to God; but in response, there is personal morality and public duty. Please don't misunderstand that, when I pick out rules for villages, I am centering on the center. The center is expressed in Ephesians 2: 8 & 9: we are saved through God's grace, apprehended by faith. Nevertheless, there are expectations about how to proceed in this life.

The Apostle Paul clearly laid out some financial rules. Everyone is expected to be productive and contribute.

> For even when we were with you, this we commanded you, that if any would not work, neither should he eat. 2 Thessalonians 3:10
>
> Let him that stole steal no more: but rather let him labour, working with *his* hands the thing which is good, that he may have to give to him that needeth. Ephesians 4:28

Then, most concerting to some:

> But by an equality, *that* now at this time your abundance *may be a supply* for their want, that their abundance also may be *a supply* for your want: that there may be equality. 2 Corinthians 8:14

However, it must be admitted, never was a government mentioned in this exhortation to giving.

There was an example, perhaps in the apex of the ideal of disciples sharing Acts 2:45 & 46, but there was also a very stern warning from God about abusing the system when God struck Ananias and Sapphira dead for lying about their contribution. Were they entering into an arrangement whereby they would be supported, but doing it unequally? Or was their fault mere lying?

There is definite direction about how people are supposed to take care of their family, including at least somewhat beyond one's own immediate family. For instance, widows should be cared for by their family. Yet, at the time the letters to Timothy were written, one without anyone under certain circumstances would still be taken care of by the church.

> 8 But if any provide not for his own, and specially for those of his own house, he hath denied the faith, and is worse than an infidel.
> 9 Let not a widow be taken into the number under threescore years old, having been the wife of one man. I Timothy 5:8&9 KJV

If one follows these personal rules, then the community rules are fairly well taken care of. But, of course, there is very much more that is taught. This improves a village for the sake of children a lot, but it does not yet cover the atmosphere of the environment.

VILLAGE ENVIRONMENT

If a group of people would follow these admonitions, they would be industrious, at least somewhat prosperous, and giving. They would have solid families committed to teaching children. If they truly committed themselves to follow Jesus as their Lord, they would be quite outstanding people. But, Jesus demands more.

> And when he had called the people *unto him* with his disciples also, he said unto them, Whosoever

will come after me, let him deny himself, and take up his cross, and follow me. Mark 8:34

Paul agrees:
> 2 Fulfil ye my joy, that ye be likeminded, having the same love, *being* of one accord, of one mind.
> 3 *Let* nothing *be done* through strife or vainglory; but in lowliness of mind, let each esteem other better than themselves.
> 4 Look not every man on his own things, but every man also on the things of others.
> 5 Let this mind be in you, which was also in Christ Jesus: Philippians 2:2-5 KJV

Such amazing people! They would not just move in miracles (Matthew 10:10, John14:12); they would be miracles.

It would be good for children. And this is what the Judeo-Christian tradition envisions, nay, commands. We are supposed to act like this. This is what God's village looks like. At the very least.

Yes, we need a village. We need a support system for the family in trouble. We need an under-girding economy for the small businessman. We need some creative and innovative thinking to solve the problems with which modernity presents us. Indeed, today we have such grace problems, we may need people with a great deal more power and insight than humans are capable of. It appears to me that we have been given that path.

How different this is from the common assumption that any child rearing that might be called Christian is necessarily about spanking, and therefore abusive. How much more hopeful and realistic is this than suggesting that government can solve the growing problem of poverty, increasing proportion of children in poverty, lowered IQ, lowered achievement, increased crime among children, disaffection among teachers, general impoverishment of governments, and gridlock among leaders?

Okay, you might say this is a fine idealistic treatment and might have worked for a small community in the first century, but is that really applicable to today? Well, to begin to cast that vision, let's update the view to our own country at its founding. What kind of private duty and civic responsibility did the founders live out, and suggest we should live out?

Founders

It is evident that the founders of the United States, by and large, practiced a Biblical religion, were mentored by leading divines; and, although they were cognizant of baser motives, hoped and prayed for an honest, righteous and civic-minded populace. George Washington prayed daily for his country, that it might be blessed with "honest industry, sound learning, and pure manners." John Adams urged upon his son, John Quincy Adams, that he read through the entire Bible each year. Benjamin Franklin was so unorthodox that he paid his tithes to an Armenian church; thus, in today's understanding, he sent his money to the Methodist church – such was his expectation of the duty of paying tithes. One of the first acts of Congress was to order a printing of the Bible "suitable for use in public schools."

Not only is it untrue that they were irreligious Enlightenment thinkers attempting to write religion out of public life, but also it is untrue that they would be incapable of understanding our situation. They were aware of adultery, syphilis, homosexuality and abortion. I am not aware of their having addressed these issues. Presumably, such issues were rare enough that then generally well known Bible admonitions were viewed as sufficient. The founders were certainly aware of corruption by government officials; they fought sharply against government intrusion. It was, after all, the Writs of Assistance (search warrants that permitted customs officers to enter and search any premises whenever they wished) and taxation (that they had not voted for) that started The American Revolution. Many wrote such sentiments as "The preservation of liberty depends upon the intellectual and moral character of the people. As long as knowledge and virtue are diffused generally among the body of a nation, it is impossible they should be enslaved (John Adams, Journal, 1772).

Civic Responsibility as Envisioned by the Founders of the United States of America

I can hear the arguments now. "Silly idealism! Could never be put into practice!" On the contrary, people who believed in civic duty based on morality issuing in liberty already put it into practice when they founded our nation. The founding fathers looked specifically at the Bible for their foundation. We can have both private and civic responsibility of this sort.

Already for a generation, by 1611, English people had been secreting Bibles around at the cost of their lives. In it was comment upon their government: God preferred republicanism over monarchy. King James I of England ordered a Bible translated so he could get the Geneva Bible out of circulation, with its anti-monarchial annotations. John Locke's father was Puritan, and this thought was passed down in political philosophy. Then the leading American Puritan preachers mentored a generation we know as the founding fathers. Even the abolitionist movement, city revivals, and temperance movement and social gospel were rooted in Biblical traditions. The Civil Rights Movement was very much, although not exclusively, a Christian movement. So, for generations, our culture was steeped in Biblical thinking, and it was this very thinking that created our nation. It is very unfortunate that this history has been hidden.

The founding fathers did not much debate policy, with regard to young children. Perhaps, in large part, they depended upon the "good office" of their wives (or relatives or slaves). They did make policies and statements regarding private and civic responsibility (as well as education, which we will take up later).

> "Laws for the liberal education of youth, especially for the lower classes of people, are so extremely wise and useful that to a humane and generous mind, no expense for this purpose would be thought extravagant." (John Adams, in McCullough)

They argued that the government could establish legal justice, insure domestic tranquility, and provide for the common defense. No doubt these help the family. Although it is not very controversial that the government should do these things, I think it may be controversial as to how well – in the last fifteen years – this has been done. What "promote the general welfare" means may be even more controversial. Education is one of those things that may rightly be considered general welfare.

Notice that the government had already made provision for public education long before Revolutionary times, but originally neither funded nor oversaw it. "The Old Deluder Satan Act" was passed in the Colony of Massachusetts in 1674, and required that any town of fifty families or more must establish a school. Although the manner of funding seems somewhat open, whether tuition or tax, the aim was clear: the population must be able to read in order to compare Bible with law so that they could keep the latter in line with the former.

Beyond some minimal "general welfare," the rest of the Constitution and the founders' writings explicitly limited the reach of government:

> An elective despotism was not the government we fought for. James Madison, Federalist No. 58, 1788

> The powers delegated by the proposed Constitution to the federal government are few and definite. Those which are to remain in the State governments are numerous and indefinite. James Madison. Federalist No. 45, January 26, 1788

> In question of power, then, let no more be heard of confidence in man, but bind him down from mischief by the chains of the Constitution. Thomas Jefferson, Drafts of the Kentucky Resolutions 1798, p. 73

Following Reform theology, if humankind is totally depraved, one could not put hope in humans continuing to do right. Therefore, there must be a structure that would restrain human will. Roman Catholic writers would have said, restrain human passion; but, Reform theologians include human will and reason as depraved, too.

> If Congress can do whatever in their discretion can be done by money and will promote the General Welfare, the government is no longer a limited one, possessing enumerated power, but an indefinite one, subject to particular exceptions. James Madison, letter to Edmund Pendleton, January 21, 1792, p. 73

Here, it sounds as if Madison would not be for socialism, progressivism, or much in the way of "promoting the general welfare." Quotes from Thomas Jefferson are even more pointed that the general welfare clause is not meant to render the *enumerations* of federal power useless. Rather, the founders meant to limit the reach of government, and particularly the federal government.

Yet, the founders knew that "the Republic must be kept," and that the work would go on and possibly change.

> The American war is over; but this is far from being the case with the Revolution. On the contrary, nothing by the first act of the drama is closed. It remains yet to establish and perfect our new forms of government and to prepare the principles, morals, and manner of our citizens for these forms of government, after they are established and

brought to perfection." Benjamin Rush, letter to Richard Price, Mary 25, 1786.

Benjamin Rush, founder of the American Bible Society, was, like his peers, envisioning only limited change and only on the basis of Biblical morality. It was a revolution in the hearts of the citizens, away from dependence on an elite and toward self governance, that he envisioned.

Policy Decisions About Children – Dream Role of Government

Let's now imagine what might be. The best society needs the least government. The worst needs the most. As long as there are fallen, depraved humans around, we will need some government, still need protection from outside threat, still need enforcement of laws, and still need enforcement of contract. How much central planning is necessary for welfare is highly debated.

Did you realize that those who think they need to take care of others are disrespecting them? Necessarily, so. Pandurang Shastri Athavale, winner of the Templeton Prize for Progress in Religion, realized this. In his effort to help his India, he did not reformulate social work or charity. Instead, he sent out his disciples to ask questions. They must not beg. They must not teach. They ask questions. From the questions that they asked, the poor farmers made a temple and each contributed to it. At the temple, they also contributed and shared their knowledge about planting. After one harvest, the temple had food to give away. The entire community prospered. Then, poor fisherman devoted a boat to be a temple, with similar knowledge sharing and distribution of contribution. Their community flourished. Questions, honest and respectful questions, were offered. The result was great change and increased prosperity. Although Hindus, His followers teach the love of God to everyone regardless of caste or economics. Specifically, He said at the outset that social work and charity were hierarchical, and therefore would never work; they could not raise up these communities like recognizing their internal wisdom might.

On the other hand, as in the case of widows in the New Testament, possibly some may need to be taken care of. It would be better if they were positioned so that they do not. Lydia did not have need to be. Many others were taken care of by a son. Some were turned away by the rules. Now, these rules are no longer recognized. So, our thinking, now rolled around as in response to some koan, is ready for a breakthrough.

If there is a need for charity, why must government necessarily control it? The more prosperous and virtuous a society, the less need there is for this function, as well as any other function of government. Further, is this not a function of the church? If we look at Matthew 25:31-46, judging sheep and goat nations based on how they treated him (naked, sick, in prison), it was on how they treated his brothers. Although "charity does begin at the house of God," I am not suggesting we limit charity to Christianity, but that Christians ought to think that charity ought to start from Christians rather than government.

I do think that originally liberals agreed to put government in charge of charity, as that seemed good in what was then a Christian nation and a government that respected a Christian worldview. Much has changed since then. Alternatively, perhaps they were seduced by the learning from the German academe, which was never informed by a successful democratic revolution but only by *"noblesse oblige."* Help, however, without respect and love, becomes control over or covert, and both Nazism and Communism proved to be authoritarian and abusive. Only charitable idealism, without bureaucratic amoralism or government control, will actually help people and raise up the masses.

Why don't we then work on transforming society? Some may not realize that such could be done; but, of course it can, and there are examples of this. Others may have some ulterior motives; they want to be in charge of the government. They think prosperity and power are zero sum games. Some might think that the shift must necessarily be so gradual that an interim plan must be instituted, but let those people show how it is interim and how it is promoting a shift.

We will take up the topic of how we can transform society in the last chapter. For now, however, let's pick up an example of how a society can be transformed based on Biblical ideas: the Welch revival. In 1904-1905, a revival broke out in Wales. A simple man prayed and encouraged his young friends to pray. Whereas the churches were previously empty, from this prayer meeting, services were established in many places, grew, and were filled every noon and night. Bibles sold out at stores. Brothels quit their business and held Bible studies in their buildings. One hundred thousand people were converted in Wales, a million in Britain, and revivals were sparked in many countries around the world, including Africa, India, and the United States. Wales was changed dramatically in only a year.

In our own country we have had similar revivals, such as the First Great Awakening, the Second Great Awakening and the City Revivals, all of which increased church attendance *and also* changed society in general. There is specific documentation of the change of young people's behavior in the First Great Awakening. There is no question that the Second Great Awakening organized life on what was then the Frontier. The Appalachian area today depends upon the colleges, churches and governments that were created at that time. The City Revival birthed abolitionism and the temperance movement, which in turn gave rise to the suffrage movement.

Our nation was explicitly founded with a vision to being "a city set on a hill," a great experiment in "the beloved community." It is time to resurrect that vision, a precisely Biblical vision. It is the only way that a good "village" can be re-created in this time.

Before we wrap up, though, let's turn to some fundamental problems normally overlooked in educational policy-making but admittedly fundamental. This is necessary so that we do not build a new system with the old problems carried over.

> Chelsea's Lunch – about government intrusion and intimidation.
> Shovels – about the high rate of unwed and/or teen pregnancies.
> Self Esteem – about an educational movement gone bad

Then, moving toward the chapter on new ideas for transformation, let's stop to take a look at a longstanding, if unpopular, method of increasing academic achievement, and how that might be applied in society and even in public schools.

Works Cited

McCullough, David. (2001) *John Adams.* NY: Simon and Schuster, p. 103.

Bible.
> Amplified
> Complete Jewish Bible
> Contemporary English bible
> KJV King James Bible aka The Authorized Version
> NIV New International Version
> Message
> Mishle
> Young's Literal
> > all found at www.biblegateway.com.

****

Please be sure to talk about *this* book
in your favorite group.

If you have a recommendation for a good character formation curriculum, please share at
www.thegovernmentisnotavillage.com.

****

Chapter Four

Chelsea's Lunch

Hilary Clinton tells us about a phase that Chelsea went through when she was young: she wanted jam sandwiches. She insisted on jam sandwiches. So, for a time, in her lunch were jam sandwiches: two pieces of bread, with jam and no peanut butter. For Chelsea, this was a short phase. Her parents decided that it was better to go along than fight it. My guess is that Chelsea is just fine having had poor nutrition for probably what amounted to a few days. Now, I have seen jam sandwiches on the menu when there was nothing else:; the bologna and peanut butter was all used up. Jam sandwiches were for the end of the month in some families. In the Clintons' story, however, a government official happened to come to Chelsea's class one of those days when she had jam sandwiches. Fortunately for everyone, the teacher did not divulge that the little blonde girl belonged to the governor of the State. She just smiled, and said she would mention it to the parents.

First Lady Clinton sort of smiles in the book at this and moves along to consider health and welfare topics, but it would have been no smiling matter to most families. Many families, in exactly the same situation, and having made the same decision about managing the situation with their child's temporary menu demands, would have been faced with government intrusion and reprisal.

I just heard the history of another favored family who had their child taken from them. Years ago, their four-year-old had undiagnosed autism. They knew he was difficult. On a preschool field trip, the child had a meltdown. The Sate took the child from the mother. She heard that they were taking him to the hospital in the Capital, hours away. She didn't hear that he was being taken to a stripped-down, locked-down "psych ward." When she followed her son, she was surprised to be detained and interviewed, discovering in the process that she was being interrogated on suspicion of abuse. Days later, this doctor's wife was allowed once again to see her child.

Today, knowing that the son had a serious case of sensory problems such that he is easily overloaded, as well as some autistic problems, we would not be surprised that a field trip at age 4 was overwhelming. Consider the mother, however, dealing with an admittedly unusual son for four years, but who now is faced with a child taken away, taken to a stripped-down, blue, locked-down, pscyh ward – for an unknown period of time. She faced interrogation. Think how difficult this was. The mother faced all this relatively alone because her husband was busy with his medical practice. Think, then, how much more difficult it would have been for a less-favored family, one that possibly would find it financially draining to stay in another town, one that might not have legal advice, who might find even childcare for the siblings back home difficult to find, let alone afford. Think of a poor woman who might not have had the gumption to follow her child or face interrogation. Wouldn't her child have ended up as a ward of the state supported by your tax dollars?

Apparently, they had to be sure that she was not abusing her son. What? How does that fit in with the story? I don't know. Why, if the child were on a field trip and "had a meltdown" there? How could that have possibly been related to child abuse at home? How was it not abuse to rip a child away from his mother and take him far away to a mental ward? Would he have been returned had the family been low-income? Parents divorced? Been minorities? Or worse, known to be conservative Christians?

Fortunately, this son and his mother did survive, and he is a competent adult. The mother has raised several children and is now doing other important work as well. Unfortunately, some stories do not end nearly this well.

Some families, unlike the Clintons, might have used jam sandwiches for lack of peanut butter. What would have happened to them? Perhaps they would not have had a friendly relationship with the teacher. They might be suspicious because they had a history of discrimination, and so be wary of teachers. The teacher might have reported the poor dietary pattern to a government official. Then, what might have happened?

Many years ago, I knew a family who decided to get a second opinion on their child's medical situation. Before they could actually get in to see the second doctor, they discovered that the State was sending agents to take the child, as if they had denied health care. Not wishing to have their child taken, the family moved immediately to another State. Amazing family. Obviously, they had two parents, a devoted mother and a father with a substantial salary. I wonder. Did having more than three children make them a target? Did they express some doubt to the doctor which was interpreted as rebellion and thereby triggered overzealous enforcement? Who endowed doctors with the right of enforcement of their opinions? What was the excuse of the government for flexing its muscles in this matter? How many families could have protected their child in this manner? How many have needed to?

How many children are taken, not because of abuse but because of poverty? One of my friends, a manager in State Child Protective Services, said that many of her staff could not tell the difference between poverty and neglect. She said that overly large caseloads and the difficulty of finding good workers meant that sometimes children were taken who should not have been. It is never good to take a child; it rips the relationship up; it scares the children. It is tragic, however, when it is unnecessary.

In 1970, when I was in high school in Bellaire, Texas, our child development class had a guest speaker from Child Protective Services who told us that, if there was ever an accusation of child abuse including the idea that the parents were conservative Christians, then CPS immediately believed the accusation and removed the child. Don't you think that society is more anti-religious today than in 1970s? Since each successive generation is more likely to favor more socialist policies, don't you think this sort of discrimination, intrusion and reprisal is much more likely to happen today? The representative told us it was standard procedure in the State of Texas at that time.

An owner/director of a child development center told me how it broke the hearts of staff when Child Protective Services would, as a policy, come during the day to pick up a foster child to give that child back to the parents or to another foster care parent. At the end of the day, the foster care parent with whom the child had been staying would come to pick up the child, only to be surprised by the fact that the child had been taken. Then daycare staff had to inform the foster care parent. Some foster parents could not take this heart pain and had to stop serving. The center wondered if maybe they should bow out too. The policy was up to the overwhelmed social worker. Clearly, it saved her time.

Frustration with government control, intrusion and abuse is rising in many sections. In Detroit, when a home has been burglarized and the inhabitants complain to the police, they lose the rest of their belongings because the police take them, claiming it is "evidence." Of course, people across the country think that the police will abuse them. In Detroit, however, they might be so frustrated and fearful that they make the first move. Even in liberal Austin, the NAACP has spent years picketing the APD. Worse, career law enforcement officers running for constable tell middle class neighborhood associations that their platform is to "stick it to the APD." The very most affluent neighborhood may not hear about it, but solidly middle class neighborhoods know that enforcement has become a problem even in their neighborhoods. More recently, two of my doctors "retired" in frustration because of government intrusion and intimidation. What hope does the common citizen have? Worse, what do the poor, beleaguered, but inquiring think? Well, to be frank, they talk about caches of guillotines, innoculation centers, and airplane-delivered toxins. They think the government wants to thin the population. So, then, how are little Chelseas and tiny Tyrones and bouncy Bettinas, who do not have a daddy in a key government position, going to cope with yet more government "help?"

Actually, the first time I saw jam sandwiches was on my first job. I worked at a privately owned child care center in southwest Houston. I was the employee that met the parents at the door and retrieved the child. Sometimes, I helped in the kitchen. A girl from the poorest high school in town was the cook. I saw Kool-Aid watered down. I was introduced to fried bologna – and jam sandwiches. Today, none of that would happen. Teenagers are not permitted in those positions in the State. Also, there are a number, a myriad, of other regulations that did not exist in those days. Some of those regulations concern food in daycares. Menus are now made to somewhat higher standards.

Today, it is not lack of regulations but the regulations themselves that are posing a health risk. Some educated but impoverished mothers complain to me that they are required to submit to having their children drink milk unless and until they can get a doctor to sign a non-compliance permission form. Doctors do not have any nutritional training, but they usually do listen to a mother who says that too much milk makes their child a snot fountain, or cranky, etc. Of course, they charge plenty for the office visit, more than a working single mother can afford. Probably, more of the population has celiac disease than realizes it. However, government regulations enforce milk. Not milk *or* milk substitute like almond milk, just milk. I wonder if it is about farm subsidies. At the same time, I have had directors complain to me in trainings that they have to spend so much time and money complying with government regulation that they wonder if they should bother with the subsidies. Some say that they think there is fraud in the new statewide corporation that has arisen to taken their worries away and help them comply with government regulations.

I guess it is hard to see this sort of picture from the governor's mansion in Arkansas. From the desk of the small daycare owner, it looks like too much government. From the perspective of the young single mother trying to work and go to college, it might look overwhelming. Back at my first job, at a little daycare that was poor in lots of ways, I didn't think about more government regulation; I wondered why parents didn't walk through the center where they left their child! It is just such cases that elicit arguments for regulation, but isn't it disrespectful to think parents cannot choose a daycare? If you were the mother, wouldn't you want the ability to choose? However, if you were a little kindergartener with the curly blond hair that had insisted on jam sandwiches – or if you were the little dark-skinned boy whose mother had only jam to put in the sandwiches -- what would it look like to you when a government agent came to your door, after having talked to your teacher, to talk to your parent about your lunch?

****

Do you have a story – a true story that happened to you or your child – that would help people understand? If so, please share it at www.thegovernmentisnotavillage.com. Thanks.

Chapter Five

It Takes a Shovel

About child rearing, Hilary Clinton says, "The best tool you can give a child is a shovel." Her father had a habit of asking her how she was going to dig herself out of whatever situation she was in, but she brings the idea up in conjunction with the problems of adolescent sexual activity.

The taproot of the problems of lowered IQ and academic achievement is the birthing of babies by parents who cannot take care of them. An obvious and growing portion of this category is unwed teens. Of course, "Many intact couples also abdicate their responsibility when it come to discipline;" however, unwed births not only affect early childhood, but might be affected by early childhood policy.

If teen pregnancy was high when Bill Clinton was president, it is much higher today. The book quotes a rate of 30%; but in 2012, the percentage of children born without a father in the home is 37.5%, and for firstborns, 43%! The biggest change is that more young women no longer think anything is wrong with having children out of wedlock.

If our media was sexualized when Tipper Gore was the Vice President's wife, it is much more so today. The sector of our economy that uses the most bandwidth is pornography. Indeed, the porn market has been maxed-out for years. It was years ago that boardrooms were filled with men trying to figure out how to involve children in a desperate bid for more profits. Indeed, as I write, I have been subjected to porn on my own computer, even though I run a professional-grade firewall, the best anti-spy-ware and the best anti-malware – as well as alternative browsers. And no one else has ever used my computer! Porn is addictive, and we can't get away from it. Yuck! We have mental sewage everywhere.

These are not merely personal problems if we are considering using public monies to pay for children's early education; and children who are impoverished because the parents cannot or will not love them, interact with them, support them and educate them adequately. We have too many children who come from such a poor background where they do not have adequate interactions with a caregiver that their brain grows appropriately. That is why Head Start was created, has demonstrable results, and why we are considering an expansion of some sort of government early childhood education. But, there might be better answers.

Even the best mother is hard-pressed to support herself and her child without a father helping. If she is young and uneducated – worse, poor – in anyway herself, she has a very difficult task. If she lives in a poor neighborhood and has a disorganized family of origin, she and her baby are certainly at risk. Few women in previous generations have been expected to cope with such situations. Extended families normally enfolded the children until the mother could remarry. Today, we are not talking about a few widows, a few unfortunately married and a few girls in trouble, but instead about many many who were never married. Young women have always had babies; it is just now they are doing it without husbands – and competent, interested villages.

It is worthwhile thinking about how we might make a competent village, but let's first think how we might ensure that baby has a dad. Biology requires a father, and we have always expected children to have dads.

If I were to quote pulpit thunderers about returning to Bible standards for sexual purity, first I would have to search through historical sermons. I have not actually heard any. Then, I would have to brace myself for an onslaught of ridicule. The thesis would be ruled out of court by the average reader as just plain silly. Maybe these two facts are related. Maybe, just imagine, if the village had certain standards that were pro-child, pro-natalistic, and somehow urged the two people who made the baby to stick around to rear it. Imagine if we promoted "just say no" to sexual urges unless there were a willingness to REAR the children. It might be possible to imagine a science fiction story in which the government required this, but the scenario seems less inviting than the imagination of a return to a simpler, more Biblical era.

Clinton says children need a shovel, suggesting perhaps that they may need to plow through a lot of BS. Her mother sent her out to face bullies, without instruction, just like stories I hear from the ghetto. Such things did not happen in my neighborhood. However, now I hear that bullies have taken over my grandsons' neighborhood playground. My grandsons are having to decide when to fight for themselves. Everyone has to fight for themselves soon enough, but it is also adults' responsibility to influence the environment. It is unfortunate if the adults in the neighborhood leave the environment to the most fierce of the young. Similarly, it is a shame if we leave the sexual playing field to the predators.

Hilary Clinton mentions her desire that teens would say no to having sex.

> I said it would be great if we could get kids to postpone any decision about sex until they are over twenty-one, which provided a round of nervous laughter from my listeners. (Op Cit. *It Takes*, p. 161)

Maybe the laughter was wan hope. Maybe it was small reaction to a not-very-funny joke. The reality is that children are making decisions about sex and gender from the time they are very young. Seven-year-olds are clearly forming gender identity. We see this when first grade girls insist on wearing dresses to school. It is a pattern separate from the surrounding culture. Just as first grade girls want dresses, boys distinguish themselves from girls early on, too.

Unfortunately the surrounding culture IS sexualized. I have seen toddlers teased about their "boyfriends" and "girlfriends" when they can hardly understand. Preschools are increasingly required to have books picturing and lessons explaining "Suzy having just two dads and Billy having two moms. " I hear stories about books in third grade picturing naked adults and explaining masturbation. Every child stands in the grocery line beside pictures of sexually displayed women. It is no wonder, then, that we also hear of school girls assaulted on playground and in the classroom.

I wish that Clinton could imagine the need for saying "no" that she urges here juxtaposed with the longstanding and widespread prohibition on saying "no" that governmental policies enforced on educators. In public education and in early childhood education, educators have been explicitly told that they must never say "no" to children. There also seems to be a trend that no one is to say "no" to the government.

For instance, I remember in 1986, when I discovered there was no classroom discipline in my daughter's fourth grade class because the principal (with a recent doctorate from The University of Texas) enforced upon the teachers that they "never tell the children 'no'." While I watched a teacher try to explain a math problem, children were standing on chairs shooting spit wads from their Bic pens. The poor teacher was not permitted to tell them to stop – and didn't, even while I was watching. Not much math was learned, but something else was. The older teachers ignored the dictate and waited for retirement, but the majority of the staff were new hires and felt compelled to comply.

My daughter complained of not having any pencils. I bought several batches of pencils for my daughter, and eventually engraved them with her name in large letters. One day in class, again with no pencil, she pointed out to the teacher which students had her pencils. The teacher told her that she was to deal with it herself. I suppose this was the teacher's only alternative because she was told that she may use only positive reinforcement. She was not to correct a student. She was not to say, "No."

That same year, I remember the day when my colleague picked up his daughter from school. She had been sitting in the office with a broken arm, crying just outside the principal's door, because she had been bullied on the playground. The principal feigned that she had not known that the arm was broken, even though the child had been sitting outside her office crying for at least two hours. We all know why there was bullying on the playground: because the teachers were forbidden to say "no."

It is the same now in early childhood. Saying "no" is not exactly forbidden in the state regulations in Texas, but any sort of negative reward is. The standards permit "time out," but licensing representatives will not. One, while inspecting my facility in the *nouveau riche* part of town, took my youngest, least-trained staff person and started grilling her on whether on not we used "time out." Fortunately, I had trained her. We didn't – at least for our toddlers. Holding a child who is harming himself or others is explicitly not permitted. It would end in a serious citation against the center, and these days, normally firing of the adult involved. Of course, that is just Texas; I am not a master of the regulations in other states, but I judge them likely more "liberal" in politics, and therefore more strict in this policy.

What do you get from a generation who never had an authoritative "no" in their life?

Saying "no" and not being able to enforce it may be worse than not addressing a behavioral problem. Teachers have been told to "redirect" for sixty years now. To many, this means tricking children. To my shock, when I was a director, I saw that some of the most intelligent and most prestigiously educated are the best at tricking children. This is not a good outcome. We are teaching children that there are no moral boundaries – and apparently that it is right to trick people.

Then, in public school, if failing is not an option because testing will be too easy or too repeated, once again, students learn that there are no boundaries.

Sounds like we are piling it up for children – and then keeping it secret that there is this neat thing called a shovel. I really do not think that this is what Clinton – or any legislator – has in mind.

> When parents are willing to take a "non-negotiating posture" on the word "no" to be strict on curfews and appropriate discipline, children are less likely to be confused about the choices they confront. (Clinton, *It Takes a Village*, p. 161)

We must teach our children to say "no." We have to model saying "no." Then we have to train them to say "no." We would like them especially to say "no" to porn. We would like them to say "no" to attacks. We would like them to say "no" to their own sexual urges when they begin to have them. But, by the time they have been trained that there are no boundaries, how is this possible?

We need to say "no" to addictions such as porn. We need to say "no" to healthy urges when expressing them would not end up being healthy, such as contracting STDs or having a baby because we are having sex with someone to whom we are not married. We might even need to say "no" to ourselves when we want too quickly and too easily to dispose of a marriage. I have come to think we should say "no" to marrying too quickly, also! How can we easily categorize all these "no's"? I fear that, if I say "traditional values," I will be immediately ruled out of court as an abuser of women and a violator of somebody's civil rights, or at least smeared as a conservative. Let's just agree that we have a problem of irresponsible sexual behavior? Hmm? Everyone from fascists to communists, pushes for more responsible sexual behavior – except for a few in the West, who can afford to play because they can depend upon society having been stable, affluent and generous.

Dani Johnson shows us how to teach children how to say "no." As a multi-level marketing trainer, she is aware of the marketing of porn. As a mother, she addressed this with her children. Then she helped us all in her book, *Grooming Children for Success* (2009). She gives scripts on how she prepares her sons to go shopping with her. What will they do when they pass by the underwear store at the mall? What will they do while they are waiting in line at the grocery?

Carol Everett showed us how she trained children to say "yes," and how we should say "no" now. She confesses publicly her history of grooming children in public schools, as early as kindergarten, to be customers in her abortion clinics. Now, at anti-abortion conferences, she tells how she was permitted into Dallas public schools, including kindergartens. From the first meeting, she insinuated to the children that their parents were ignorant, couldn't help them with matters of sexuality, and that she and only she could be their competent friend in such matters. In what passed for "developmentally appropriate ways," she encouraged sex in order to sell abortions (http://prolifeaction.org/providers/everett.php).

By the time children reach puberty, they already have made many decisions about sexuality: what it means to be a boy/girl, how to handle those of the opposite sex, and much about how to handle sexuality. Our culture is HIGHLY sexualized. Children see and are directly taught poor models of sexual relations. Adolescents are seduced, enticed, and forced into sexual relations. Not addressing this situation is abetting it. Clinton is clear on her concern about teen pregnancy; but today, after fifteen years of policies more or less like hers, the statistics are far worse.

We could say "no" to an overly sexualized culture. Tipper Gore tried to do so in a public way by focusing on ratings. While the United States enforces a ban on child pornography, the UK expands anti-porn laws now to requiring child-friendly filters on all internet service providers unless the adults choose to turn them off. Iceland goes further, banning all printed and internet porn. Too often, such efforts are passed off as hopelessly reactionary or anti-liberty. The ACLU takes up the worse porn cases with the idea that, if they pick the worst, then the kind of free speech that the founders envisioned, of religion and politics, would be well protected. First, I doubt that is true. I have seen a president stifle dissent about an expensive and ill-planned war. I have read of inexpensive, effective therapies being shut down, raided and run-off. I know of numerous instances of religious speech being squelched by government officials. By contrast, porn seems to be generally well-protected. Porn is as addictive as crack, harms familial relationships, and yet is protected as if it were a public good. We could at least remove it from times and places where children are likely to view it.

Children see poor examples of sexuality – and are increasingly directly taught them. A friend of mine told us about her young mentee. The child asked her (a retired professional with distinguished bearing) how many men she had had. My friend explained to the child "Only one. Only one man for me." The child said, confidently and disapprovingly, "Now, that just won't do." Perhaps her mother needs as many relationships as possible for better economic chances, if all of them will be shallow and temporary. Alternatively, perhaps her mother thinks it is prowess to have several relationships at once. Clearly, the child has no concept of her older mentor's much more affluent lifestyle and values, yet she felt she should teach her mentor. Why did she have so little reference point that she felt confident that she should correct the older, much richer woman?

What is being taught in school? Sex education continues to be very controversial. Biology lessons are common. A few schools address the topic of how to handle dating relationships. Some schools go so far as handing out contraceptives. There are a few schools where sex education is not taught. Liberals cannot understand the assumption that teaching about sex and contraceptive encourages sexual activity. Conservatives cannot understand why not. They ask why liberals do not see the direct connection between teaching that sex is healthy and that there are means to prevent conception other than abstinence and an increase in sexual activity and in teen unwed pregnancy. This is not the time to solve that debate, but I will observe that we have had sex education in most public schools since I was in them in the 1960s. Mostly, we have taught a biological approach to sex education; and for that time period, we have had a rising rate of sexual activity and unwed pregnancies.

Incidentally, most of the churches that offer sex-education offer a variety that is very liberal. The Unitarian Universalist Church promotes a curriculum that includes how-to instruction on masturbation. Most churches, by contrast, do not mention the subject, even in terms of how to choose a spouse. There are some curricula available now, but few encourage abstinence. The Mennonite/Church of the Brethren curriculum, by Debbie Eisenbise and Lee Krahenbuhl, is the only one that I know of that focuses on mutual respect and Scriptural foundations, rather than on only encouraging the view that sex is healthy or preventing abuse.

Will it soon be considered discrimination if educators do not teach homosexuality as an accepted way to express sexuality? To the extent that publically funded schools teach sex education, likely this will be the stance. What about private education? While I was a director of a licensed childcare center in Texas, I attended the local AEYC directors' meetings. NAEYC, National Association for the Education of Young Children, is the *crème de la crème* of accreditation, considered to name the best centers in town. The publicly paid "mentor" of the group told us that we must have in the classroom at all times at least one book that introduced the idea that Johnny might have two mothers or Suzy might have two dads. Further, we must have a unit in each classroom each year on the same non-bias topic. I was amazed that the directors in the room, nearly all of whom were directing a church-affiliated program, said nothing. I thought surely the controversy would eventually erupt. Later, when I conducted a thorough search, I could not find this requirement in the AEUYC literature. Where I found it was in other accreditation standards, such as Rising Star, that more centers ran to when there was a fear that they could not obtain AEYC accreditation. Directors of Christian centers complain to one another in private groups now, but they feel powerless to act against a government that they see powerfully stacked against them.

Further, as a trainer, I see that, in many states, each and every training must be thoroughly checked by the state authorities – or some outsourced authority. Never, at any time, is a trainer approved, but only each training. Now, given that I still see many very poor trainings and I still see very unscientific claims, it is my opinion that what is being strained out is "traditional values." Christians are suspected of being abusive because they may believe in spanking. Further, they will be suspected because traditional ideas of sexuality and marriage may be considered discriminatory. Indeed, in Texas, soon ALL evaluations will be funneled through one website, thus ensuring that, if any single participant complains of bias, discrimination or abuse, then very quickly the trainer will be shut out from being able to train at all.

The government may thus enforce a pro-sexual, even pro-homosexual, curriculum. Expanding government's control over early childhood will finish the plan to oust any notion of traditional sexual restraint.

It would be lovely and poetic to be able to say we need to say "no" to ... certain things we are taught are immoral ... but we cannot say that today. Increasingly, we are not permitted to "say no." We would be accused of discriminating and taking someone's rights away. But look, one person's rights end where another person's start. It is right to protect the rights of the minority, but it is also correct to enforce the will of the majority. It is not correct to take away the rights of the majority in the effort to please a minority. That would be a tyranny of the minority. Further, it is not possible to have a stable society on rights only. We must consider duties – particularly duties to children.

We need to be able to say "no" to unwanted sexual content in our environment. Right now, we have such piles of it that we need heavy equipment, not shovels! If we, the citizenry, cannot say "no," then it is no wonder that our children are not saying "no."

The lack of transparency illustrated by the ongoing storm about the Common Core Curricula and the flap about the CSCOPE curricula being secretly written under the auspices of the Regional Service Centers in Texas are examples of the citizenry not being given a chance to say "no." This sort of political maneuvering shows disrespect to the citizens but also to our founding principles of self-governance. Particularly when it comes to having sexual content enforced upon us and our children, we must be able to have a right to "say no." We have had a policy of forced over-sexualization in our whole society, including our schools and now increasingly in our preschools.

It is time we said "no" so that our children will have the opportunity to do so. This is not merely a Malthusian point for reducing population. We simply cannot solve problems with the mindset that created them. We have created a rights-only, entitlement society, and cannot solve the problems but only exacerbate them with the same ideas.

It was my guess that the changes in NAEYC accreditation were instituted because of Hilary Clinton's 2008 candidacy for president in order to make existing high-quality center personnel the likely hires in the new public school system. Perhaps this would bring up the low quality of pre-K education – or not. However, the expansion of the pro-homosexual curricula was successful, in any case.

Of course, I am not accusing Hilary Clinton personally of supporting policies that encourage inappropriate sexual behavior and subsequent social problems, but I do notice that existing policies and programs are not having the desired result. The statistics have worsened. Observe that the sector of society where Head Start and other government support programs are the most common is also the sector where there is the highest rate of unwed pregnancies. Could it be that the direction of causation is opposite to what we assume? As unpopular as it may be, given that perhaps government's policies and programs influence people's behavior, maybe we need a re-thinking.

For instance, today on NPR, there was a dialogue of some young women concerning the sexual behavior of some "stars." One argued persuasively that, yes, we should judge and call out public behavior that models behavior that would be harmful to any normal young girl, even if we don't judge someone's personal private choices. Another argued that, no, it was an attack on womanhood to criticize a female star's sexual behavior – of any sort. Then the conversation focused on how race and gender were alike – or not in terms of rights. WAIT! STOP! Reader, please do your own evaluation of the logic patterns here. Consider the values that are permitted to be foundational: rights, protected classes, non-judgementalness. The good of children, which was the original topic of conversation, was quickly off the plate when non-discrimination and rights came up.

We have a highly sexualized society; we have sexual behavior slopped over everything, which is negative for adolescents, their babies, all children and the wider society. This is not being addressed in churches or homes, and government policy is abetting the problem.

Clinton seems to have only two answers. One, parents should have a non-negotiating stance on curfews in an authoritative way; and two, we should encourage sex education in schools. She argues that there is no evidence that teaching sex education causes promiscuity. She does not cite evidence for good results, nor does she distinguish between kinds of sex education.

Once again, we see how dramatically these answers fall short. Families, of course do need to take up their first duty of teaching children. Unfortunately, governmental policy is often at odds with this. Traditional values of keeping sex within marriage for stable families worked for millennia; yet this government, education and the marketplace view this as somehow hayseed and ridiculous.

Churches need to take more responsibility for supporting the family, but their heretofore pitiful efforts have been so ridiculed and maligned that I fear to write such a thing. Simply calling for spanking and non-divorce, left off decades ago, would be ridiculously inadequate. We need a new breed of leaders who can model, mentor and teach a more fulsome message. We need some stand-up educators to sort out good from bad, sound the alarm politically, and implement sound policies. We certainly need some statesmanlike leadership.

Each of us should weigh our demands for our own rights against the needs of society's children. If we want to have fun, want to make money, or want to assert our right to differ from what has always been the moral norm, we must begin to first consider our duty to support child-friendly, majority-friendly policies. Otherwise, we are enemies of our own future. There may or may not be a right to engage in non-standard sex; but there is certainly a right to not have it in our children's faces.

Once society can say "no," it is possible that children can learn to say "no" again. Only then will it be reasonable to expect young people to say "no" to natural urges until they can be responsible parents. To get ourselves out of where we are, we have a lot of digging to do.

It should be abundantly clear, however, that any government policy without a societal change and robust families will at best fall short. Nevertheless, further government intrusion, teaching the very things we all say we are against, is foolishness writ large.

Chapter Six

Self-Esteem, Self-Evaluation, and Judgment

We have a large problem in education today of low achievement (apparent test scores notwithstanding). Part of this is due to basic demographic problems (poverty, single parent households, and differential fertility rates), and part of this is due to poor instructional practices, but some of it is due to a misguided self-esteem movement. Today, students in the United States think of themselves as the best in the world; they have the highest opinion of themselves. No other country has students who would rate themselves as highly. It is not a pretty picture to be arrogant, even if one has a correct assessment. Given that our achievement is the lowest of any industrialized nation, however, we have some problems. Obviously one of the most immediate problems is lack of self-application. Entitlement is rife. Entertainment is demanded. Lower achievement has been the result of the self-esteem movement.

One of the problems of the movement may have been that the term was never adequately defined. It may have been that the first coiner of the term was Morris Rosenberg in the mid-1960s (Baumeister 1996), who defined it as personal worthiness. Then, it was thought to be a predictor of higher achievement. This seems to make sense because a person who thinks of themselves as a good student, for instance, finding that they are not making a good grade, would probably work harder to be sure to make that grade so as not to have cognitive dissonance. Their confidence in their ability spurs them on to self-application. But, that is my thinking. Instead, A. Maslow is often cited, who in his hierarchy of needs theory based on kundalini, suggested that, without the need for self-esteem being met, the individual would never achieve self-actualization. For Maslow, self-esteem had to do with obtaining the respect that we deserve. Carl Rogers, influential humanistic psychologist, grounded his famous unconditional love as therapeutic technique in the idea that many people thought themselves unworthy of love. He said:

> Every human being, with no exception ... is worthy of unconditional respect of everybody else; he deserves to esteem himself and to be esteemed (Bonet).

Given that this quote has been cited by those continuing to promote the movement, amazing as it seems, it appears that the claim is that everyone has an inalienable right to a positive self-evaluation regardless of behavior. Is this not an end-run around the basic notion of moral judgment or reciprocal ethicality? It is hard for me to believe that the movement in our public schools was grounded in this notion. If this does characterize the philosophy, it is no wonder that we have the results we have.

On the first day of a college freshman level class, I give out a survey of three or four questions. The first question is, "In the Civil War, who or what was the Union?" This is the easiest social studies question I can construct. In Texas, the Civil War is in the curricula in the third, fifth and the seventh grades, and then again in high school American History. So I would expect a college freshman to say, "The North." Usually, only about half of my students can answer correctly. In the next class meeting, I give the answers to the survey, and alert the students who didn't know the answers that they need to inquire if they have the prerequisites to be in the class or to allot more time for studying. Later, we use the data to compare sections and discuss how we lay out data. I remember so clearly the day that one of my students, a 17-year-old young lady, informed me that my telling the class that they should know the answer to "what was the Union" by the time they were college freshman was hurting their self-esteem.

Her complaint and remonstrance was genuine and heartfelt. However, I think, if she really had had good self-esteem, if she had thought that she were a good student, she would have merely redoubled her efforts to study or she would have ignored me as a difficult teacher. Instead, she took it upon herself to correct me, with emotion, in public. Somehow, to her, I was acting immorally.

Most American students rate their ability highly; however, I do not think they really have high self-esteem. Instead, I think they expect educators and parents, and thus the world, to cater to them. They are immature and unskilled, not just in academic matters but in character. Some are jaded, others just inured to boosterism.

About three years ago, it got worse. Across the college and across institutions, professors noticed a change. Students were even less engaged and more demanding. Failure rates went up significantly. One of our colleagues who taught in both public schools and colleges explained it to me: when No Child Left Behind Came back to Texas, the Texas legislature mandated that there would be no end to "re-takes," and that there was a lot of hassle for a teacher before one could award a failing grade. I had high school students in my classes who explained it similarly: since no one could fail, poor students did even less, teacher morale went down and so did that of the best students. Being on the attendance roll started conveying the expectation of passing. Then this expectation was carted to college. Since up until now this is not the professors' expectation, failure rates skyrocketed.

And yet, students come in saying that never has schooling been as hard in Texas. When I ask them why they think that, they respond that their high school teachers tell them there has never been as much testing. Do you see the logical fallacy? Yes, there has never been as much testing, but never have we taught at such a low level.

There has been a movement for at least yermyu years to boost self-esteem in children. Why did this ever get going? Baumeister, et. al., trace the literature to California Assemblyman John Vascocellos arguing that raising self-esteem in youth would reduce crime, teen pregnancy, drug abuse, school underachievement and pollution (p.1); but, even after nine years of meeting, his committee had no evidence to support their claim.

To date, the research is spotty, contradictory and problematic. First, all the research depends upon self-report, which thus skews not only reported self-assessment but also assessment of others and one's life circumstances. For instance, some people are "down on" everything, thus appearing that they have both low self-esteem and poor life conditions, whereas neither may be accurate assessments if taken objectively. Secondly, even should a correlation be found, the direction of causation is not found. For instance, being successful in school might cause higher self-esteem, rather than higher self-esteem causing better success in school. Third, studies show that self-assessment of skills, popularity and beauty do not have much basis in reality. Perhaps more important, although Baumeister, et. al., do not mention it, the operationalization of self-esteem may be clumsy. There may be more than two kinds of self-estimation, low or high. Rather, there might be very low, healthy, and overly high. Alternatively, there may be different kids of positive self-assessment healthy and unhealthy.

At any rate, while studies are mixed or contradictory, the original theory that increasing self esteem in youth will reduce crime and teen pregnancy, and increase school performance has not found any support. Instead, Baumeister's review suggests that "perpetrators of aggression in general hold favorable and perhaps inflated views of themselves," that those with high self-esteem are more likely to break off relationships, and those with a heightened self-worth are more likely to demand preferential treatment or to exploit their fellows" (Ibid passim). Baumiester, et. al., conclude: "We have found little to indicate that indiscriminately promoting self-esteem in today's children or adults just for being themselves offers society any compensatory benefits beyond the seductive pleasure it brings to those engaged in the exercise" (Ibid.)

The whole idea that we should lavish praise on children in order to raise their self-esteem has been strongly corrected in scientific literature and in popular literature since the mid 1990s, but nevertheless is still being taught in early childhood teacher training. So preschool teachers, those most forming our children, still are taught to praise children. I do not find any seminars on how to correct children, and almost none on how to teach skills of self-application or self-restraint. I still see a call for self-esteem seminars. Little has changed from the height of the movement.

Martin Seligman is a leading scientist in how children build self-esteem. He does original research and has for decades. He writes for the general audience. Martin Seligman shows that only achievement increases real, healthful, self-evaluation. Only real achievement!? Therefore, while of course running children down and making them think they can never do anything right is not wanted, neither is empty boosterism. Kindly leading children toward better achievement and giving praise where praise is due is what creates self-esteem – the kind that is healthy and leads to higher achievement.

Here is how Seligman illustrates it for the parent:

> A boy does poorly in a baseball game. If Dad says, "You're great," the boy is further unhappy because he knows that is bunk. If the Dad says, "I know you tried hard and let's throw the ball around in the yard and prepare for next game," then the boy will be happier.

How, then, is it, that teachers are still being told to praise, praise, praise? The idea has been drummed into teachers for so long, everyone believes it. When faced with contrary evidence, now trainers are urging that educators be specific. This is entirely insufficient. The calls for science-based training are disingenuous when it strains out anything else but this discredited doctrine.

What happens now is that, every time Johnny paints something, it is praised. Every time Suzy runs around the room, she is told she is *so* fast. Johnny knows that this is just something teachers say. Suzy may be entirely unprepared to discover that LaTanya runs faster than she does. We still have the old self-esteem movement.

Neither is a return to simple-minded praise based on competition sufficient. Some children are talented at one thing and others at another thing. It is all well and good to recognize and celebrate these differences; but, if we use these as the praise that children get, this is not (1) loving them for who they are but for what they produce; and (2) does not motivate achievement. Indeed, it is the lament of leadership coaches than very often the most talented people in any given field never reach their potential due to lack of discipline and self-application. If we praise Johnny because his painting is best when he just happens to be the most talented, this might build up arrogance but not self-esteem that, as Seligman has shown us, is built through achievement.

Bright and talented children also need help to develop maturity and achievement (van Gemert, Mensa Bulletin August 2013 p. 20 following Cskzentmihalyi, Gelb, Sternberg & Williams, Smutny and von Frem, and Mora). Just because they can easily solve problems that seem advanced for their age, this is not sufficient for the need for creativity in the world. Being able to focus and solve problems everyday is needed in the world. Geniuses, too, could use help in developing their greatest potential. Both intelligence and creativity can be developed. "It turns out that creativity can, and often does, partner with constraint and deliberate intention" (Van Germet , Lisa "Creating Creative Children. Mensa Bulletin, August 2012 p.20). "To be effective creatives, children must be taught that prolonged effort is not the opposite of ingenuity; it is its superfood" (Ibid. p. 21).

Praising a specific action or talent is hardly better than rather slopped-over praise of all. The one is a bad counterfeit for personal love, and the second an entirely bankrupt substitute for real motivation for achievement. Neither is really based on science. It would have been better had we been taught, "Say something nice to children." That might have helped. Instead, we were taught that any correction was harmful. We were led to believe that, if only we could lead children to more self-love, then they would be .... somehow better. The experiment has gone on for a long time, and the results we see are the reverse. Children are not nicer, more peaceful; teen pregnancy is not down; the juvenile crime rate is not down; and although pollution has subsided, I doubt very much if self-esteem is the cause.

Why does this happen in an environment where all ECD training is supposed to come under the scrutiny of being scientifically based? Every single seminar must be approved by the State, and nothing that is not scientifically based is supposed to pass. Yet, the old self-esteem movement, which has given us a generation of lazy, arrogant and demanding children, and lowered practical and academic achievement, is still passed despite the fact of longstanding science contradicting it. Why? We all know that the State is trying to sift out anything that might be religious and traditional.

Common sense suggests that people do not need help in loving themselves and in thinking of themselves highly. Rather, people with the best teaching may aspire to loving others more and to behaving ever better.

What does the Bible say?

> *Let* nothing *be done* through strife or vainglory; but in lowliness of mind let each esteem other better than themselves. Philippians 2:3 KJV

> And to esteem them very highly in love for their work's sake. *And* be at peace among yourselves. I Thessalonians 5:13 KJV

> For I say, through the grace given unto me, to every man that is among you, not to think *of himself* more highly than he ought to think; but to think soberly, according as God hath dealt to every man the measure of faith. Romans 12:3 KJV

These Biblical admonitions correspond with common sense. People need to be encouraged to aspire to better behavior, caring for others. The entire group needs to be encouraged in giving honor to higher moral achievement.

Of course, an overly low self-estimation that causes someone to not try is strongly taught against through the basic idea of faith in the empowering of God. Nowhere here is there any hint that self-loathing or self-condemnation is encouraged "There is now therefore no condemnation" (Romans 8:1).

Further, I have heard many a mention from the pulpit, when reading Romans 12:3, that we should not think of ourselves too lowly either. The doctrine of "I am a worm" is historical, but even then, centuries ago, was balanced out by the grace and election of God. Further, in every doctrinal strand of Christianity, there is a striving toward better performance – and part of that is getting along with others.

It may be that coming out of the Victorian or Edwardian Era, there was some overly strict child-rearing, and such discouragement as to embolden psychologists to say, "Don't be so hard on yourselves." However, no one looking around today can suggest that people being hard on themselves is common. Rather, we all know that, from children to adults, people see themselves in the best light possible, shift blame, and increasingly do not aspire to good citizenship, let alone moral excellence or saintly altruism.

The practice of the self-esteem movement of praising children indiscriminately to the exclusion of correction has resulted in (1) lack of the kind of self-esteem that contributes to higher achievement; and (2) an increased kind of negative self-love that fails to love others. If an enemy had come and stolen our youth and brainwashed them to this extent, we would raise up in arms and fight until we reversed the situation or until we were all dead. Americans are like that. But, instead, we have done this to ourselves, cooked our own frog in a slowly boiling pot.

The self-esteem movement must be dismantled, and quickly, and replaced by scientifically based self-talk that increases practical and academic achievement. At the same time, a movement needs to arise and be given space that teaches Biblical, time-tested moral aspiration. We are likely so far removed from the morals and politics of our founders that it may not be realistic at this time to suggest that the Bible be the text in our public schools (as they did when the Continental Congress published for use in schools a Bible, and when founders promoted the New England Primer that was chock full of Bible). If I were to suggest such a thing, that in itself might be reason enough for many to throw this book away. Surely, surely, however, Biblical principles must be permitted in Christian and privately owned early childhood centers and schools. At this point, however, nothing of the sort is permitted in most colleges, any public school, or in teacher training for pre-school educators.

Fortunately, we do have some scientific works that suggest we that may be closer to the truth. Vygotsky and the Kozminskys have shown us that appropriate conversation with children can help them develop social and internal skills. Vygotsky has argued that social interaction is the primary thing that builds cognitive skill. He is the founder of the work on "scaffolding" for infants and toddlers.*

Carr & Borkowski, Clark & Artiles, Dweck, Fosterling, Kistner, Osmore and LeVerrir, Lizminki & Kozminksy, and Wiener all have shown how attributional dialogue improves learning. In general, this method trains teachers to dialog with children in such a way that responsibility is realistically framed. Thus, when classroom results are not as desired, children easily see that exerting any effort, the event can be modified. Here are some conversations that are illustrative.

Before:
A paper with a poor grade is handed back. Teacher says nothing. Child says to self, "This subject is hard," or, "I stink at this," or, "This teacher is stupid."

After:
Teacher: "Mike, I noticed that your grade was not high. What happened? Did you study?"
"I don't understand."
"What can you do when you do not understand?" (Guiding question.)
"Ask for help?"
"Right. So who is responsible, you or the difficult material?" (Guiding to responsibility.)
"Of course I am, but it was too late."
"What can we do now? "
"Can I stay after to study this and take a re-test?' (Progress is personal.)
"Yes. Great idea. Make a list of questions for me and I'll be glad to help you. (Details strategy.)
Do you see how this celebrates achievement rather than giving empty boosterism? This research parallels that of Seligman. Both examples are for elementary school-age children in order to be a bit more illustrative, but the principles are the same in the early childhood classroom.

Contrary to what we have been taught about praising children, even for specific actions, we need to first love them for themselves; and encourage development, and celebrate it when it happens ,or build steps or scaffolding for achievement when it is not yet happening.

This motivational attributional style does suggest a kind of healthful positive self-esteem. A student who knows that they can change the outcome of circumstance and has a mentality of success, when faced with possible failure, will resolutely make the changes in order to ensure success – consonant with their mentally held identity. This kind of success can never come from empty boosterism but only from earned achievement.

Seligman grounds his discussion of the optimistic child in his or her discussions with parents. There is plenty support for teachers successfully encouraging academic and social success with modeling attributional styles that frame responsibility. However, this is directly contrary to the empty, repeated and specific praise that early childhood teachers are still taught through government enforcement.

The best situation is a couple of parents who give that deep love to their child and are personally invested in the achievement of their child, and who will work with approbation and correction to see a powerfully competent adult that has good respect for others. This is the aim of the traditional Judeo-Christian tradition. These teachings have had good effect in both Jewish and Christian homes. It had a good effect in the early history of our own nation. In the early 1900s, however, the New England primer and its Biblical morals were supplanted. Horace Mann responded to critics of his reform by promising to let the Bible speak for itself, but he is now credited with removing it from the classroom. John Dewey aimed at balancing child-centered freedom with delivering knowledge, but his reforms resulted in a racist and classist system. Philosophy, reform, regulations and practice conspired to press secularism on us and to disallow anything that smacked of traditionalism. Then we had experiment upon experiment, with the self-esteem movement being one of the most long-lasting ones. Without a grounding in real science, but with the support of those using science as a supposed bar to traditionalism, it has given us now more than a generation of people with inflated ideas of themselves; entitled, without humility, and in assessing their own abilities too highly, without self-application for achievement.

If we put even more government control over early childhood, we will have nailed the coffin shut. The government as it is now controls every bit of teacher training, every bit of educational philosophy, except what can come out around the edges in small, privately run centers. Since we have seen that a parent's home or a church-affiliated school is best, and since we have seen that government policy is wrong-headed and government-run schools are far worse, how could we be duped into letting the control be total?

Accurate academic evaluation itself is stymied. Nowhere is judgment more attacked than around moral judgments. Schools lead in this change of society. Government policy has created entitled, low-achieving people through the self-esteem movement, continues to do so; and continues to bar the better, more scientifically supported traditional character formation.

Works Cited

Blark, M.D., & Artiles, A. (2000). A cross-national study of teachers' attributional patterns. *The Journal of Special Education* 34(2). 77-89.

Baumeister, R.F., Campbell, J.D., Krueger, J.I. And Vohs, K.D. "Exploding the Self-Esteem Myth" *Scientific American* Dec 20, 2004

Baumeister, Roy F.; Smart, L.; Boden, J. (1996). "Relation of threatened egotism to violence and aggression: The dark side of self-esteem." *Psychological Review* 103 (1): 5–33. doi:10.1037/0033-295X.103.1.5.

Bonet, V. (2014). Sé amigo de ti mismo: manual de autoestima. 1997. Ed. Sal Terrae. Maliaño (Cantabria, España). ISBN 978-84-293-1133-4. http://en.wikipedia.org/wiki/Self-esteem#cite_note-Bonet-15 retreived Feb 7,2014.

Carr. M. & Borkowski, J. G. (1989) Attributional retraining and the generalization of reality strategies by underachiever. *Human Learning and Individual Difference,* I, 327-341.

Csikszentmihalyi, Michaly. (2008) *Flow! The Psychology of Optimal Experience.* NY: Harper Perennial Modern Classics.

Dweck, C. S (1986). Motivational processes affecting learning. *American Psychologist*, 41, 1041-1048.

Forsterling, F. (1985) Attributional retraining: A review. *Psychological Bulletin*, 98(3), 495-512.

Gelb, Michael. (2000). *How to Think Like Leonardo da Vinci: Seven steps to genius every day.* NY: Dell.

Kistner, J., Osborne, M. & LeVerrir, L. (1988). Causal attributions of LD children: Developmental patterns and relation to academic progress. *Journal of Educational Psychology*, 80, 82-89.

Kozminsky, E. & Kozminsky, L. (1995). *The effect of learning strategies and attribution training on the reading comprehension of high school students with learning disabilities.* Research report. Ben-Gurion University of the Negev, Beer-Sheva Israel

– (2002) The dialogue page: Attributional dialogue for improving learning motivation. *Intervention in School and Clinic,* 38(2), 88-95.

– Improving Motivation Through Dialogue," *Educational Leadership.* Sept. 2003

Mora, Pat. (2010) *Zing! Seven Creativity Practices for Educators and Students.* Thousand Oaks, CA: Corwin.

Popham, James. (2001) *The Truth About Testing.* Association for Supervision and Curriculum Devel., NY.

Ripley, Amanda What Makes a Great Teacher? *The Atlantic,* Jan/Feb 2010. Among the findings in Teach for America of what predicts a great teacher from a poor one is relentlessness. Often teachers give up on their students.

Sternberg., RJ. & Williams, W.M. (1996*) How to Develop Student Creativity.* Alexandria VA: Association for Supervision & Curriculum Development.

Smutny, Joan Franklin, & von Fremd S. E. (2008). *Igniting Creativity in Gifted Learners.* Thousand Oaks, CA: Corwin.

Weiner, F. (1986). A*n Attributional Theory of Achievement, Motivation and Emotion.* New York: Springer-Verlag.

Chapter Seven

What Kind of Education?

If you recall, Clinton wished to address the problems of low IQ, low achievement and low health, high crime, and high teen pregnancy caused by poverty and broken marriages. She did not address the interlocking nature of these problems, and only hinted in the book at government intervention. In reality, she is offering us "the solution" of government-controlled daycare, probably rolled into the public school system. Before we hand over our children and tax money, we should ask what kind of school ends up in higher achievement and better behavior and success in life?

Although the results of Head Start are widely touted, the fact is that Head Start as a program has been shown to increase achievement only for children from very low-income backgrounds. Head Start programs showed no improvement for more middle class children. Further, even with these poor children, the effects of the Head Start early childhood education proved temporary, lasting only a few years. By grade six, these children were on the same track to failure as their peers, at best; at worst, Head Start offers no advantage (Coulson, DHHS, Darcy, GAO).

This is not to say that early childhood education does not raise academic achievement or IQ, or that it could never theoretically improve ethical and practical behavior. Please notice the assumption in Clinton's book that all early childhood education is the same. It is not. HeadStart is not on the same high level that most church-affiliated schools and some privately owned centers are. Corporate centers tend to be somewhat better than government programs, but typically never as good as the more established, mainline church-affiliated schools. Cursory visits to representative locations will reveal this – even to an untrained eye. As a trainer and consultant in the industry, I can tell you that Head Start is not interested in buying training for its teachers; the folks who invest in high-quality, high-content training are first the mainline, church-affiliated schools and secondly the owner-operated schools. Head Start does offer their own training. Those seminars assume participants are illiterate. Training often consists of games; and then, at the end, participants are given the words to fill in the blanks, which is considered the test. There is not much content at all. For instance, when I went to ITRS training, led by well-qualified trainers flown in from across the country, I found that, while we had fun dancing and singing, no one in the group could tell you at the end what ITRS was. Everything I learned about it, I read – while not listening. This experience is illustrative. There may be some variation given partnerships, but overall, HeadStart invests much less in teacher training than other forms of early childhood education do. Probably most HeadStart programs offer an experience better than the alternative of no education for poor children in the worst neighborhoods, but that is not the point for our purposes. Our question is which kind of educational opportunity is best for "every child." HeadStart is not of the highest quality.

Neither is pre-K. Public school teachers are not given education in whole child development. They simply are not presented with the same curricula in college that early childhood educators are. That is why, at least in the universities I am familiar with, public school educators and early childhood educators are trained in completely different departments. Public school educators are trained specifically in order to fit them for our (failing) public schools. Further, most pre-K classrooms are set up specifically to reach out to the poorest families in town. They have higher teacher/student ratios than the law allows in licensed CDCs, far fewer toys, a lot more regimentation, and lower expectations. I know of no data on their success. After all, public schools depend upon testing to verify their achievement, and that kind of testing begins at third grade. Overall, public school early childhood education violates the two most fundamental principles in early childhood education: curricula should be whole child and developmentally appropriate. Public school was not designed to teach whole life skills, but only academics. Pushing academics downward through the grades is not developmentally appropriate. Further, the worksheet approach is not developmentally appropriate; it is neither effective nor efficient. It is, of course, very profitable for textbook publishers. Young children need a hands-on, multi-sensory and individualized approach that is foreign territory to a system designed to process the masses.

Nor does all early childhood education have to be group education. Options of care by the mother, perhaps given curricula as Comenius envisioned, or in the home of a professional as is permitted in the Family Day Home Option, or by relatives, are all more natural. Studies conducted long before electronic indexing showed robustly that children who stayed at home with their mothers had higher IQs than those sent to CDCs. Recently, no such study has been conducted; first, because the finding is inarguable, and also because today such a finding would be very unpopular.

There are dangers to bringing groups of very small children together. Germs spread like the plague – literally. Today, the literature is replete with studies on this topic. Government institutions, unlike parent-run groups and privately run businesses, will not have sufficient interest in reducing the spread of germs because there is no legal liability. For instance, hand-washing is very much enforced in daycares. By contrast, today, few public elementary school have provision for the students to wash their hands even before lunchtime. Installing an alcohol sanitizer on the wall is more common. This is inappropriate, in the first place, no one supervises its use and children have been known to get high or ill on ingesting it. Hand-sanitizer is sometimes illegal in CDCs due the the possibility of a child getting high or ingesting it. Secondly, it does not clean nearly as well as does soap and water. Thirdly, it leaves toxic residue on the hands. This is only one small detail in a myriad of details about cleanliness and low pollution that is vitally required in group care, but ignored by the government.

Moreover, the safety of small children thrown together with older children who are unruly and dangerous is very often not adequately addressed. Further, studies show that even five-year-olds are stressed out at being put in large schools. While this can be reduced by having the children delivered to the door of their classroom rather than to the playground or lunchroom, it still remains a concern. Corporate daycares expanding in size may be of concern, and certainly placing small children in public schools is even more a concern.

Even in terms of academic achievement, the move toward public school is wrong-headed. If we are aiming for high academic achievement, then the very last thing we should contemplate is sending our children to public school. United States public schools have for some decades now been at the bottom of the heap of industrialized nations, and increasingly are below that of many developing countries. High-stakes testing has deceived many parents into thinking that achievement is up when it is really down. SAT and similar scores were re-centered downward. Popham (2001) has disclosed how these tests have gotten easier and easier in order to look better and better. I notice that the new STAR system in Texas is no longer norm-based, but now only criterion-based, taking away the last hope of comparing the achievement of Texas students. The Asian and South Asian parents in my metro area are enraged. Everyone else seems to be entirely fooled. Our nation's educational system has entirely failed and is not making strides to improve. How could we consider putting even younger children into it?

Particularly has the public education system failed in three fundamental area: in teaching Math, language arts, and even more in teaching comportment. All of these begin very fundamentally in the earliest years. Here, the public school has adamantly been going in the exact wrong direction. Math is taught as badly as possible, using worksheets instead of manipulables. Once the need was discovered, worksheets were instituted at even younger ages! Imagine, taking away the toys from the three-year-olds and four-year-olds, where they might learn through their senses how math and physics work, and instead making them sit at tables, together, slaving over worksheets! Similarly, spelling has been taught about as chaotically as possible. Have you ever seen any curricula that build English spelling in an organized fashion? That teaches the patterns of English spelling (other than mine)? Yet, we wonder why our students do poorly! Then with the focus on the math-based disciplines, the teaching of not only spelling but also reading and writing, up through analytic and synthetic reasoning, have further eroded. The greatest failure of all is the lack of teaching comportment, practical self-management. Even more than the lack of STEM/math ability, employers complain that graduates have no idea how to comport themselves. This is because such teaching has long been outlawed in public school. By now, any teacher who remembered traditional values being taught in school has retired. The teachers and administrators themselves cannot model proper comportment. For instance, let me tell you about the second grade teacher in a local elementary school who encouraged the class, in unison, to ridicule students who did not read well out loud. We could talk about the junior high school faculty member who gave tests answers to students on their State tests as they were proctoring. We might consider the Assistant Principal at Lubbock High who made a practice of pulling chin hairs off of students. Somehow, I doubt any of these folks know about the comportment taught in the New England Primer!

Neither Head Start nor Pre-K in public school has much claim to fame. By contrast, based on meta-analysis, William Jeynes (2003) finds that religious schools outperform on academic achievement. Of course, the best schools in any locality are church- or synagogue-run. Contrary to popular thought, it is not because they have better students, bigger budgets, more money per student, or even primarily because the families are more affluent. What about the non-elite schools? Religious schools, *and religiously committed students*, **on average**, outperform *because of greater self-application*. Jeynes agrees with the common researchers' explanation that because these schools were designed to form character, they stimulate self-application and end up with higher academic performance. This result is obtained even when the schools were not originally designed to outperform on academic achievement.

This point is so significant that it bears repeating. While a great deal of law, money and attention has been bearing down on public education, results have been grim at best: on average, spiraling downward. By contrast, the religiously affiliated schools outperform. The finding is robust. The finding is not simply because income in the home correlates with academic performance. The finding is not simply because many church-affiliated schools aim at higher academic performance, although some do. Expectation of the surrounding adults does predict academic achievement. However, this meta-analysis that Jeynes offers goes further. Even schools that are founded for other, more religions purposes end up with higher academic achievement. Researchers suggest this is because the character formation inherent in religious purposes ends up with the happy result of higher academic achievement.

Parents who want the best academic outcome for their children are already investing in religiously affiliated schools. Public schools should take a lesson, and adopt character formation programs and cultures. Government must reverse policy of making it hard on religious institutions. We must not adopt the policy of placing ever more of early childhood in government-run institutions. We must certainly not, through our governmental policies, run church-affiliated preschools out of business by enforcing a broader governmental control over the education of every child.

Clinton's book is often misquoted; younger women regularly assert that placing children in daycare raises IQ. Neither Clinton nor any authority ever asserted such, yet this has become the common idea. Then, with a concern to raise academic achievement, there has been a push to expand government-controlled early childhood education. The likely result of this will be the opposite. Further, with direct, uneven, prejudicial enforcement, religiously affiliated preschools are targeted by licensing representatives. Then, with apparently unrelated policies such as Obamacare, religiously affiliated schools are having a hard time complying with policies that do not match their reality and are considering closing. We need a warning bell as loud as an air raid siren. We must not continue in the direction we have been going in terms of educational policy. No nation will be great without an educated citizenry. Good educational result will not happen without good character formation. Good character formation will not happen if our Judeo-Christian heritage is despised. Our serious problems will not be solved by unclear, emotional slogans. Our problems will be greatly exacerbated by more, similar governmental programs. Let us not turn over our money and our children. Let's return to the heritage that worked well. It was a specifically religious heritage, with room for diversity, but united in basic principles of Judeo-Christian character.

Works Cited

Andrew J. Coulson, (2010) "Head Start: A Tragic Waste of Money," *New York Post*, January 28. http://www.downsizinggovernment.org/hhs/subsidies#_edn14.

Darcy, Ann Olsen. (2000) "It's Time to Stop Head Start," *Human Events*, September 1.at: http://www.downsizinggovernment.org/hhs/subsidies#_edn11.

Government Accountability Office, (2000) "Preschool Education: Federal Investment for Low-Income Children Significant but Effectiveness Remains Unclear," GAO/T-HEHS-00-83, April 11, p. 7. http://www.downsizinggovernment.org/hhs/subsidies#_edn12.

Jeynes, William. (2003) Religion, *Education, and Academic Success*. Greenwich CT: Information Age Publishers.

U.S. Department of Health and Human Services, (2020) "Head Start Impact Study: Final Report," January. http://www.downsizinggovernment.org/hhs/subsidies#_edn1.

Chapter Eight

Ideas for Transformation

The argument that only a return to strong adherence to the Judeo-Christian religion ethic seems so culturally despised that I would fear to make it, except for a conversation I had. It was a Mensa New Year's Eve party. In a circle of about eight of us, with me being the only Christian, it was agreed by consensus that our society was in so much trouble that only a revival would save us. I hope that this effort, a mere dialog in best childcare policy, has helped educate us on our choices.

Get Educated

Education is a fine place to start, however insufficient. I am shocked to discover that I may now be classified with Phyllis Schlafly! Somehow, the book *Who Will Rock the Cradle?* came to me while I was writing this book. It is composed of articles by experts arguing that daycare is a philosophical necessity for a socialist agenda to tear apart society and harm children.

> With respect to children under two years of age, the evidence of researchers is unanimous: being separated from parents, and especially mothers, for an extended period of time on a regular basis seriously weakens the child's attachment to his

mother, and this weakened attachment results in damage to a child's emotional and intellectual development.... It is precisely in the top-quality center that research demonstrates that daycare is risky to the emotional and physical health of children (Schwartz, 277 in Schlafly).

But, it is a total illusion that any such "quality" daycare could be created across the whole nation of the United States. It's a completely quixotic, crazy idea that the kinds of commitment which women make for their own children can be reproduced in large numbers of public centers ... Child care is a competitive issue, it's a productivity issue, it's a moral issue, and it's a religion issue (Gilder, 164 in Schlafly).

Perhaps this is why a University of Maryland study recently concluded that crime rates can be better predicted by the percentage of single-parent homes in an area than by the socio-economic class of the resident ... Unfortunately, children raised in one-parent households are far less likely to make successful marriages as adults than peers raised in two-parent households ... (Christensen, 184 in Schlafly).

This book came to me because I was involved in this project. I would never have read it in 1989 when it was published – because I was *educated.* Indeed, reading a sentence like Schwartz's on p. 271, "Making the state responsible for the care of small children is the *sine qua non* for socializing the family out of meaningful existence," even today causes me to wonder what the problem is. Isn't the family the center of oppression for women? Only after remembering that single-parenting was not very freeing do I come back to today's argument. We must have a change of society for the good of children; and to do that, mere academic education is insufficient.

Believe

If we are going the wrong way, the thing to do is to turn around and go another direction. If we have problems beyond our ability, then the thing to do is to believe in miracles. Fortunately, we are offered some.

I have been entirely reasonable in my arguments here and supported them with documented science. My conclusions have led to a Biblical morality. We might have given testimonies of blessing for the moral. We might have witnessed the power of God. I encourage your exploration, adherence and commitment to Love, Truth and Beauty – in short, God and that manifested as Jesus the Messiah.

Alternatively, if I have persuaded you that Judeo-Christian values dispersed through society would benefit children, then please let me suggest that you become the change you wish to see.

Believing is a fundamental first step to doing. People don't do unless they believe.

Do

Some people do believe, and are doing. Let me give you some examples.

Given the robust evidence that church-affiliated schools out-perform, every church ought to invest in a home educators' group, a child care center, and a school. Each ought to have some scholarship spots. Indeed, perhaps all of their tithing members ought to go for free? The rest of the spots are mission spots aimed at serving the community.

Then, we ought to be in the business of taking back public school. What I mean is that those who are concerned about Judeo-Christian character formation should not abandon the project of public school.

Of course, we must foment change in a way likely to work, and thus perhaps not the most angry and obstructionist way possible. Seven Mountain thinking is not entirely new; leaders in society – back to Washington? Constantine? Moses? or Abraham! - thought that godliness, virtue, and character, learning and leadership went together. No leader, not even David and Solomon, have led in a society entirely homogeneous. Nevertheless, they led with consensus values. These values included some and excluded others – those that would tear down society, hurt the whole. At no time should the well-being of children and hope for the future be traded for some mesmerization ostensibly about pluralism but in reality about accepting evil, even by the most besieged minority.

Other states ought to follow Texas in liberalizing policy regarding home education, making private education a right, so that they can have a better-educated population and better comply with American values, quite aside from the fact that it lowers their expenses. Home-schooling parents, you know, still pay the property tax in Texas, although they shoulder the expense of educating their own children. Given that they also very much outperfom academically, a state is really ... lacking sense ... if it resists home education. Unless they have other outcomes in mind.

A number of churches are working to provide after-school programs. The Church After School Association, Inc. is a non-profit, United Way agency out of Tupelo, Mississippi, that is providing subsidized after-school care. The Baptist General Convention of Texas has a document posted on the internet on how to start an after-school program in one's congregation. In Austin, the For the City Network is a consortium of churches engaged in a number of pro-child initiatives, including promoting families to foster and adopt, and an after-school program in poorer Austin elementary schools.

The Stoller Foundation's Nabor Houses concept is a Christian answer to Head Start. Essentially, to top-quality early childhood education, built in partnership with foundation funding and existing communities, two special elements are added: first, conversionary

Protestant values; and secondly, a cohort for the children. HeadStart graduates lose the advantage they gained in the program over time, but Nabor House children will go to public school with a cohort that will confirm both character choices and academic achievement. These elements will ensure a better outcome than government programs.

Cedar Park Kiwanis and Knights of Columbus have adopted the local Bagdad (Road) Head Start. For twenty years, they have been giving their time and money to support quality of life for poor children in the program. Smith noticed children standing outside without coats one winter day. Members read and tell stories. Last Christmas, they raised $2,000 for new toys. Up until last year, they also performed maintenance on the HeadStart building, since federal funding has always been insufficient. Even though it has been cut further and the club is smaller now, they continue to support the center.

Kiwanis is a service club that has children as its priority. While they are not a specifically Christian club and do have members from many faiths, their objectives include giving primacy to human and spiritual rather than to material values of life, to encourage living by the Golden Rule, and to develop a more serviceable citizenship. I spoke with Mr. Carl Starnes, who personally has started many Key Clubs in local public schools here as well as the Sun City Kiwanis Club, now the largest in the district.

Early Act First Knight is a character-formation curriculum written by Randall Parr. He noticed that while 36 states had enacted bi-partisan legislation asking for character education in schools, little has been done. His curriculum includes respect, personal responsibility, honesty, compassion, fairness, tolerance and service to others, using the pageantry of chivalry. The program consists of 10-minute messages to be used daily in school, locally selected service projects, and a reward ceremony complete with knight regalia. First Knight often teams up with Rotary, which promotes service to the community; it has an existing Early Act program to urge young students to engage in such. Rotary often makes grants to schools to purchase the program.

If Carl Starnes or Randall Parr can get things going, so can a woman. Alice Lloyd came from her native Boston to the hills of Kentucky, in hopes of improving her health. In 1916, she founded a school for the bright but poor students of the Appalachian area. The college, which now bears her name, continues to offer free tuition for students from its area in exchange for work. It boasts second place in the nation for having the least debt and 23rd in the nation for the highest alumni giving. Mrs. Lloyd's motto was, "The Leaders are Here." Her aim of preparing Christian leaders by preparing students for professions continues there in the hills of Kentucky.

Another woman saw a need in a faraway land, and her initially small action is causing large effects for women and for children. Patricia King, xpministries.com, saw extensive sex trade in Thailand. Her response was to offer to set up a young woman in a laundry business. King bought a bag of soap, printed some stationery, and offered some instructions. The young woman now had a business washing the sheets that others were still enslaved upon. Today, the woman has a business employing several other women. Now, these women are free and are able to support their children, who in turn will not have to be sold into sex slavery. King offers mission opportunities to people in high-income countries to help in similar circumstances.

Probably most ministries have some sort of outreach to poor children. Not only is this a good and right thing to do, but also they know that doing so bends the heartstrings and opens wallets. Well, and good. It is part of human nature to want to nurture children. May there be many more.

There are probably many other worthy initiatives, but this handful give us some hope and example.

Go

Therefore, if believing and acting are important, then the next step is doing something. Christians were sent out with the command from the risen Lord to GO into all the world teaching. Teaching children, being an advocate for children, and being the sort of village or society that is good for children surely is part of that vision.

Dream

Child-friendly policy is not something that can start and end with government policies and programs. We must ourselves live lives that are child-friendly. Some of us may not have children, and perhaps just as well, but we must all consider children – assuming we want a future.

Once, I was making a decision and my parents (World War II generation) were urging a particular course of action with regard to my career: I was having too much concern for my daughter, I was told. Then, I had a dream in which someone was serving me barbecue. It was particularly sweet. Then, I saw it was barbecued baby. YUCK, to the max! I decided that I ought to favor my daughter's well-being over my career.

At my 40th high school reunion party, someone surprised me by declaring, "You won!" Given that we had a very large high school, I was meeting mostly people I did not know. We were all sharing what we had done. Although in a funk, not being at all satisfied with my extreme efforts, small success, abundant persecution and general poverty, I tried to recount a short history in good spirits. I was startled, then, when this wealthy psychologist exclaimed, "You won!" What could she possibly mean? She said that, if I had a good daughter and well-adjusted grandsons, this was more important than a high-flying career. Apparently, most people in her world had the career and money, but were disappointed with their children's outcome. While any victory I claim is based on grace through faith, I think her evaluation of success is very thoughtful. What we do with the next generation counts for a lot. Maybe we all need the barbecue dream?

In another dream, I was running through a large building, rushing to get on with the ministry project. In a hurry and thinking I knew the building, I took a shortcut through an office. To my horror, I found a series of high tables on which were laid out live, drugged children, ready for dissection. What was I to do? I had to get out of there before I was found. My previous project became unimportant. I had to help these children. I had to get out, though, and quickly. I resolved to get help, to come back, to relieve the children of their suffering.

We are in this spot today. Children are suffering. Some in poverty. Nearly all are in neglect of parental love and guidance. Quite a few are in group "care." Most are in a failed educational system. We cannot improve our society and the lives of our children using the same philosophy and methods that brought us to this sorry place. A better path is well-marked. Let us change directions. Let us *become* the village we wish for our children. Let's take the same path our founders trod, lit by the Word of God.

Please come to www.thegovernmentisnotavillage.com to tell us about the great ideas that your community has implemented. Tell us how it has helped children, their families, and our society.
Thank you very much.

****

Special FREE Gift from Author (More than $258.97 Worth of Pure World Changing Information)

Sharon Sarles offers you an incredible opportunity on HOW you can change the world.

Childcare Center Directors, Principals, Pastors others :
  Advance in your career.
  Get away from deceptive nonsense into what really works.
  Discover the secrets to improve your work group culture
  Serve children the way you always wanted to.
  Be the salvation of society – well, okay, an extension of the Lord's.

by getting on Sharon's newsletter for her Director clients.
Includes discounts on Sharon's books.

TWO free months test drive with only one-time charge of $5.95 to cover postage. Then you have no obligation to continue at the lowest Gold Member price of $99.97 for the rest of the year. ($120.97 Canada or International). In fact, should you continue with membership, you may still cancel at any time.) And of course, it is impossible to lose, because if you don't absolutely love everything you read, you can cancel after two months and not owe a penny. (Offer good one year from publication.)

TIME-LIMITED OFFER: ONE YEAR FROM PUBLICATION

Plus 3 Free Reports, if you will accept them via email.

- **How Employees can Steal and How to Prevent it – report worth $50.00. (Yes, clients such to pay $50 for this report.)**

- **How to Shop for Health Insurance – report worth $50.00.**

- **How to Make Money While Doing Great Evangelism: Daycare – report worth $39.97.**

Name_____

Church/School/Business_____

Address_____

City_____

State_____ Postal Code _____ Country_____

Phone _____fax_____

email_____

Signature _____ Date_____

Enclose $5.95 for postage, and send to Sharon Sarles, Organizational Strategies at P.O. Box 971, Cedar Park, Texas 78613.
Providing this information constitutes your permission for Sharon Sarles to contact you regarding related information via mail, email, fax or phone.

OTHER Information FROM THE AUTHOR

SPEAKING ENGAGEMENTS, CONSULTING, MEMBERSHIPS: information at www.orgstrat.net. Direct contact to Sharon's office: fax 512/249-7629.

Other Books by the Author

Swim with the Dolphins, not the Sharks: Peace Skills – secular conflict reduction book.
How to Win the Game of School – study skills for community college students.
Learn at Home for Great Shalom: Faith Family Method – for homeschoolers.
Don't Lose Your Faith During College, Loose it – for the college student.
God Wants you Healed – complete with Bible Study and personal stories of healing.
Legacy Workbook – Bible study guide for leaving a legacy in your children.
How to Contend for Your Children – Bible study workbook on praying for your children.
Prayers for Great Shalom for Your Children – prayer guide.

CDs

- *God's End-time Advice to Educators* – 4 CD set, 7 messages
- *God Wants Healing, Health and Wholeness* – 1 CD 3 messages
- *Self Esteem : Unraveling Nonsense* – 1 CD, 2 messages
- *The New Audio New England Primer* – 1 CD

Ask for an entire catalog of Sharon's work from info@orgstrat.net

ANYONE: Tell five friends about this book and get a pin that says, "The Government is not a Village."
Just give proof you did this (photocopy your letters or copy your emails), and send us your land address.
P.O. Box 971 Cedar Park, Texas 78630
sharon@thegovernmentisnotavillage.com
(Through 2015, while supplies last.)

Help us out.
Join the discussion at www.thegovernmentisnotavillage.com
and spread the word every way you can.

www.ingramcontent.com/pod-product-compliance
Lightning Source LLC
Chambersburg PA
CBHW032007080426
42735CB00007B/534